THE FLOWERS
WHITBREAD
Rugby World '95

THE FLOWERS
WHITBREAD
Rugby World '95

NIGEL STARMER-SMITH
AND IAN ROBERTSON

Queen Anne Press

A QUEEN ANNE PRESS BOOK

© Lennard Associates Ltd. 1994

First published in 1994 by
Queen Anne Press, a division of
Lennard Associates Ltd
Mackerye End
Harpenden, Herts AL5 5DR

A catalogue entry is available from the British Library

ISBN 1 85291 552 8

Edited by Caroline North

Printed and bound in England by
Butler & Tanner, Frome and London

The publishers and editors would like to thank Colin Elsey of Colorsport for
providing most of the photographs for this book.

Thanks for additional photographs to C. Henry, David Gibson of Fotosport,
Allsport UK, Colin Whelan and Ian Robertson.

Thanks also to Whitbread for their continuing support and to Cathay Pacific,
The Hongkong Bank and Save and Prosper for their contributions
to this year's edition.

CONTENTS

COUNTDOWN TO THE WORLD CUP

by LEO WILLIAMS, Director of Rugby World Cup 1995

The kick-off at 2.30 pm on Tuesday 25 May in the game between the host union, South Africa, and the defending champions Australia, will mark the commencement of one of the greatest contests in contemporary world sport. Looking forward, at the beginning of September, 1994, we have only eight months or so before Rugby World Cup 1995 in South Africa.

It will mark the end of more than three years of planning, preparation and mental and physical effort by the directors and executives of the Rugby World Cup companies and by the myriad of financial, legal, commercial and media advisers who have been working with them. The effort required has been monumental. The commercial programme is on track; the media programme still requires a great deal of work.

Many rugby followers and even a number of administrators strenuously opposed the IRFB decision to award the tournament to South Africa, a country with an almost total void in international contact for the last 20 years. So far events have supported the IRFB. SARFU and its president and executives, Louis Luyt and Riaan Oberholzer, have spared no effort in meeting their side of the bargain reached with Rugby World Cup. Emerging from the rugby wilderness they have worked incredibly hard to ensure that the 1995 tournament will be an event which leaves an indelible mark in the pages of rugby history.

However, there are still obstacles to be overcome to ensure that the tournament runs smoothly and the reasonable expectations of the competitors, the rugby public and the media are met. There will be, of course, detractors. It is an unfortunate paradox of modern society that despite best efforts, best intentions and high-quality organisation, some are interested only in promotion of dissension and division.

For the 16 fortunate participants the prize at stake is more than the William Webb-Ellis trophy – more

David Kirk, captain of New Zealand, winners of Rugby World Cup 1987.

Nick Farr-Jones, captain of Australia, winners of Rugby World Cup 1991.

than the right to be called world champions. It is the ultimate prize of national self-fulfilment on the rugby ground. The spoils of the victor will be measured beyond possession of a magnificent gold cup. Rather will they be measured by an upsurge of interest in rugby by national development and by a whole generation of young people who aspire to a place in their international team for Rugby World Cup 2003 or 2007.

On the way through, millions of people in all parts of this world of ours will be treated to the spectacle of rugby at its finest, and the memories will linger and the debates will continue long after the last beer and long after the dust settles.

This is the world of rugby – may it live forever.

THE END OF THE GAME?

by IAN BEER, Immediate Past President of the RFU

Ian Beer, former captain of Cambridge University and England international, former headmaster of Harrow School and past president of the Rugby Football Union.

Extract from the Presidential Address to the Rugby Football Union on 8 July 1994.

There are two aspects of rugby which could ruin the game – violence and the misuse of money.

The RFU entertained the International Board last autumn and I urged the board then in my speech that they have to face up to those problems. I received no response at that time, so I took the opportunity in the heart of Pretoria in the presence of Dr Louis Luyt, the president of the South African Rugby Football Union, to explain why I was concerned and I painted a scenario for the future of the game if the game were to go professional. By professional I mean players being paid for playing the game. Players may, of course, make money by activities off the field as permitted by current regulations, and I am happy about that. My scenario for the professional game, if you pay them for running on the field, goes something likes this:

1. At first all is well but then you begin to lose one or more players who do not want to be paid employees. They will follow their careers in their own professions and are not prepared to sign on the dotted line and be at the beck and call of the union whenever the union so wishes. In the main these players will tend to be players from the professions, i.e. doctors, lawyers, barristers, teachers, service officers and so on. They may play instead to a high level as amateurs, just as ex-American footballers, having left college, have turned to amateur Rugby Union rather than continue as professional American footballers. I can see the amateurs of England playing against the amateurs of Wales in the warm-up game before the professionals take the pitch and I know which game I would prefer to watch!

2. As a consequence there will probably be a greater percentage of players who may be on a bonus to win and, devoid of the spirit of the

game, they may resort to violence. This image, already in evidence, will begin to destroy the game and I am sad beyond all measure that both Phil de Glanville and Jonathan Callard should have been unnecessarily injured in my year as president. If such injuries are allowed to go unchecked there will be no game left for parents to encourage their young to play. Tour agreements limiting the period for citing to 12 hours made it impossible to punish any player for injuring de Glanville. We requested that the word 'wilful' be removed from Law 26 (c), but to no avail. The fact that the New Zealand manager was dismissed and the coach reprimanded on their return to New Zealand was small comfort. The investigative committee which we requested to consider the circumstances of Callard's injury has sat in South Africa and a further meeting of the South African Disciplinary Committee was held in July.

Dr Louis Luyt, president of the South African Rugby Football Union, host to Rugby World Cup 1995.

3. In this scenario you then begin to create a limited number of power bases in the game with money; players move to these bases, induced by cash and you destroy loyalty to the less financially powerful clubs. Games then are won or lost according to the bank balance.

4. You begin to undermine the voluntary commitment of a lifetime's service to the game and slowly the type of person who administers the game over all the country changes to the possible detriment of the spirit of the game.

5. You then begin to find it difficult to find people who will coach the young and pass on the values which you and I have inherited from our predecessors. The coach will want to be paid but the money may not be there as it will have gone to the players, who may be demanding more and more, and to the match officials, let alone to administrators.

6. Finally the freedom and independence as a governing body to run the game as you wish is lost as you become a slave to sponsors, the media and the spectator. He who pays the piper calls the tune, unlike our present situation, where our sponsors could not be more supportive and wish to protect the nature of the game as we know it today.

We will then have lost the game as we know it in England and you will then have to decide whether or not we have let down our future generations because of our inability to stop the tide of professionalism. One hundred years ago, the Rugby Football Union stood firm and the Rugby League was formed. I wonder what you all want to happen between now and the turn of the century? Your voice could be very important. The by-laws of the International Board, the body which controls our game, state that 'the game is an amateur game ... it is a game played by amateurs'. Yet we are told that players in many parts of the world are being paid for playing and sometimes receiving bonuses for winning. The present situation is not fair to any of us. It is not fair to players, who are being kept amateur to the best of our ability. It is not fair on our administrators who, are pilloried for not accepting professionalism. Rarely are we praised for supporting the by-laws of the International Board. It is not fair on those who feel they have to cheat in order to achieve whatever objective they have set themselves.

To go professional is, in the short term, the soft option. In the long term it may be a very wrong option. We have a World Cup to play next year. Are the participating players to find that some are paid whilst others are not? The competition becomes a farce.

I therefore ask the International Board, as a matter of extreme urgency, to decide either that it really wants this great amateur game to stay amateur, in which case it must take immediate action, or that it announces that the game will go professional. To continue as we are is dishonest. If they were to decide to keep the game amateur, a first step could be to demand of all countries who wish to participate in the World Cup that they sign special declarations that no player in their country will be paid for playing rugby throughout the calendar year of 1995. The second step would be to decide how to enforce the IB by-laws after that date.

So ends another presidential year, and if you detect sadness in my voice you would be right – sadness that I move out of the presidential chair but greater sadness because I know I leave for my successor a game in danger of tearing itself apart at the top through money and/or violence or both, and one which requires very strong leadership across the world.

For me at least I now know that those who have been seriously injured are likely to be better cared for by the supporters of the game, whatever else is happening in rugby football. When I become jaundiced by certain events on the international scene I think of the hundreds of clubs up and down our land who are living exponents of the spirit of rugby and I cheer up.

REFEREEING IN CRISIS

by FRED HOWARD

Referee societies throughout England have recently been asked by the new national referee development officer to take stock of their membership and to put forward development plans for the future. The results have not made good reading: some societies have as much as 70 per cent of their membership in the 40-plus age bracket and only a trickle of new recruits wish to join. Why is it that societies are finding it so difficult to attract new members?

Well, the job is not what it used to be. When I began to referee over 20 years ago refereeing was very much a social activity in which the referee was seen very much as an integral part of both the game and post-match activities. Even at senior level it was not the done thing to openly criticise the referee. Mistakes were tolerated on the field and soon forgotten afterwards. Rarely was the referee mentioned in match reports and even less often criticised. Sure, there was foul play in the field, with personal feuds often taking place owing to the familiarity of the fixture lists, but these were soon forgotten afterwards and jugs of beer were the order of the day. In short, the game was a social pastime in which results were largely secondary to friendship and camaraderie.

Discipline is essential, even in a friendly. Fred Howard finds it necessary to send off Milan's Fabio Gomez as Leicester entertain the Italian side at Welford Road in September 1993.

How times have changed! The greatest tenet of refereeing had always been that the referee was the sole judge of fact. What he said went and even if he clearly made a mistake it was all part of the game and accepted with little show of dissent. Touch-judges were usually club members of some maturity, press-ganged into the role with the promise of free beer for the evening.

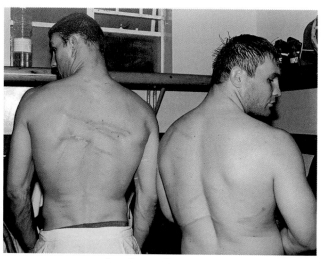

Unacceptable injuries: Lawrence Dallaglio and John Hall (above) and Jonathan Callard (below) after England's match against Eastern Province at Port Elizabeth.

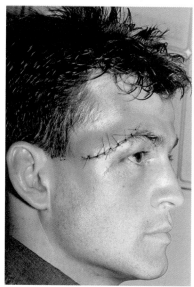

Today, with the increased presence of television and the availability of video replays, the referee is no longer the sole judge of fact. Any player who is dismissed is now permitted to take along a video recording of the incident should it suit his cause and the disciplinary committee may take this into account. You may feel this is a positive development but nevertheless it has changed the nature of refereeing and has played a part in reducing the authority of the rugby referee which for so long has been the envy of so many other sports.

There is no doubt in my mind that refereeing at all levels, not just in the sports shop window, is in deep crisis. Violent outbursts by players are increasing, with punching seen as almost acceptable in some circles. The use of the boot on the prone player is widely accepted in some countries if it helps to free the ball on the ground and some well-documented serious injuries over recent seasons have ensued. Not only that, but some ridiculously lenient and inconsistent sentences have been dished out to the miscreants. How can you explain to the local junior player who receives six to eight weeks' suspension for punching that all is fair when an international player, acting as captain of his country, is told that a sending-off was sufficient? The answer is that you cannot.

Many captains of sides at all levels now think that they have the right to question a referee's decision or at least to ask for clarification. They have no right whatsoever: the law is quite specific in that it states that they must retire ten metres immediately and allow the opposition to take a quick penalty if they so wish. What the dissenters are doing, of course, is deliberately slowing down the game and allowing time for their own defence to realign. Not only that, but they are helping to undermine the authority of the referee in the eyes of both players and spectators.

It is becoming more and more common for a referee to

find himself involved in criminal proceedings. Three times in the last couple of years I have been asked to attend court to act as both a character and an expert witness in cases of alleged assault on the rugby field. But more importantly, referees are now being cited as having been negligent when players have been injured during a match. The RFU have found it necessary to take out insurance to cover referees for this contingency, but who wants this threat hanging over them every time they take the field for what is still, for the majority, a social physical exercise?

Recent law changes have not made the job any easier. It is now virtually impossible to police the offside law effectively either in open play or at second phase, where there are so many other things to look for. There is no doubt that recent developments in communication between referees and touch-judges are helping in certain areas but such experiments are only in their infancy and require more refinement. In any case, some of the touch-judges appointed in England have limited experience and the assistance they can offer is therefore limited.

Throughout the world the international referee is under more scrutiny and pressure than ever before. It is not uncommon for a leading administrator to contact local rugby journalists to ask them to write a feature about areas of an opponents' game he is unhappy about in the knowledge that the feature will be read by the visiting referee. It is believed that this will help focus the referee's attention on those areas and so assist the home team. How many times in recent years have we seen a referee change his whole style and emphasis between matches in a Test series? Quite a few, I would suggest.

As money has a greater and greater influence on both the game and its participants so this is bound to affect the referee. Senior players in certain countries are now making vast amounts of money from commercial enterprises associated with the game. The England team now travels with its own fund-raising agent and profits are shared amongst the players. In some countries some referee societies have insisted on jumping on the bandwagon and are demanding quite substantial match fees, which are being paid. There is no way, as some people believe, that this will improve the standard of refereeing. What it will do is attract people into the job for the wrong reasons; it will also further diminish the authority of the referee and the respect shown by players towards him.

Just as the game itself is at a watershed, so too is refereeing. Many issues need to be urgently addressed if we are to continue to attract quality people into the job. Love him or hate him, no one has yet found a way to play the game without the referee.

IT'S NOT LIKE IT USED TO BE!

by PAUL ACKFORD

Not so long ago rugby was an easy game to understand. Come Saturday afternoon eight forwards were supposed to spend 80 minutes fighting a bunch of similar desperados to provide the ball for one of seven backs to score. The piano-shifters grunted and grovelled for the piano-players to hog the limelight. That was how it was and had been since the Dead Sea was just sick.

You knew where you were in those days. Forwards were big, mean-looking blokes who frequented murky, unlit corners of bars. The tall ones were called props and they pushed in the scrums. Any other misfits who did not slot into either category were usually the psychopaths who belonged in the back row. Each player had a specific job to do and was judged on his ability to deliver the goods.

It was basically the same story amongst the backs, although the differences in physique were less marked. Not any more. Nowadays international forwards are expected to be competent across a whole range of skills. It is not good enough simply to be a ball-winner. When the appointed time comes the very best players are also competent ball-users.

Imagine the scene. Ellis Park, 24 June, the World Cup final. Five minutes to go and England are three points adrift. Suddenly Will Carling slips his marker and hurtles towards the line with only the full-back to beat. Carling wants to make sure. This is no time for heroics. He slows to let the support get to him. Up lumbers the giant Martin Bayfield, all 6 feet 10 inches of him. Carling fires out a poor pass, knee high. Bayfield stoops to gather it but knocks on and the prospect of sporting immortality gurgles down the plug-hole once more.

Any sympathy for Bayfield? Not on your life. He may have made 13 consecutive two-handed catches in the line-out to get England into the position to win the World Cup, but cometh the hour and he blows it.

Five years ago, it would have been well done for getting there, marvellous fitness levels for such a big man, but all that is taken for granted now. From full-back to prop, rugby players have been forced to become omni-competent. It is no longer good enough to be master of the scrum or line-out if that is all a player has to offer.

Remember the fuss when Jeff Probyn was axed from the national team for Victor Ubogu? All the pessimists looked into their crystal balls and expected to see the England scrum retreating at a rate of knots. Instead the scrum was steady and Ubogu added a bit of bite to the loose play. Ubogu is the future, a player who can offer a range of skills to a team. The days of the specialist are numbered and we are beginning to see the emergence of an identikit forward who is all things to all men.

Australia learned that lesson a long time ago. That is the reason why they won the last World Cup and why they will still be the team to beat four years down the line. Australia are evolving a team which is rugby's equivalent of Johan Cruyff's great Dutch soccer team of the 1970s. For total football read total rugby, players skilled enough to fit in whenever and wherever required.

John Eales is a prime example, a man rated by most good judges as the pre-eminent line-out specialist in the world. That would be enough for most people, but not Eales. He has recently played in the Super-10 series as a flanker and – incredibly – was the first-choice goal-kicker in some of

John Eales, one of the new breed of multi-talented forwards.

the matches. That kind of all-round ability allows Australia to play any kind of game. In the wet and the mud they can shut up shop, ask Eales to concentrate on providing top-drawer line-out ball and control the game through the tight forwards. On bone-hard pitches with a touch of sunshine, switch Eales into expansive mode and you have a lock who is capable of playing fast and loose in an unstructured game.

Eales is a one-off, a freak athlete, but that kind of flexibility is essential in modern rugby and it is something that most European sides – with the honourable exception of France – are struggling to emulate. England are getting there. They have discovered a nucleus of forwards who could play anywhere in the back five positions of the scrum and not look foolish. Martin Johnson, Nigel Redman, Ben Clarke and Tim Rodber are all blessed with a range of skills to do damage in the tight and

Victor Ubogu on the rampage against Ireland in February 1994. In support are fellow forwards Martin Bayfield, Neil Back and Steve Ojomoh.

contribute effectively in the loose play.

It is not just a matter of the forwards getting it right. The Australian centres, Tim Horan and Jason Little, at their best tackle harder and maul more ferociously than most international flankers. It is taken for granted that they can pass, kick and perform all the other chores required of midfield backs.

All the pundits point to the undeniable flair and finesse of Jeremy Guscott, but his greatest asset is that he combines that breathtaking talent with tremendous defensive abilities. In 1989, when he was playing for the British Lions against Australia, Guscott was caught miles from safety by the Australian back row. He managed to hang on to the ball until his own cavalry arrived, whereupon he handed it on to a forward only to see that player lose possession. The match was played in Sydney, yet you could have heard the torrent of abuse Guscott heaped on his team-mate in Brisbane. His own mauling skills were far superior to those of the supposed specialist.

Such is the vision of rugby in the 21st century, and it is not all that appealing. In the old days, under the old laws, it was somehow comforting to be able to differentiate between positions and scenarios. A stand-off was meant to dance around a bemused prop, who grabbed thin air as the number 10 flashed by and looked a right pillock. These days it is just as likely to happen the other way round.

RUGBY WORLDWIDE

THE IVORY COAST COME OF AGE

by CHRIS THAU

Warriors from the land of the elephant, welcome to the big world scene. The unthinkable has happened: Ivory Coast, regarded until June 1994 as one of the curiosities of international rugby, have come of age in spectacular fashion, knocking out the original favourites, Namibia and Zimbabwe, to qualify for the World Cup in 1995. Their comprehensive win over Zimbabwe, by three tries to one, on the final day of the African qualifying tournament in Casablanca must rank as one of the biggest upsets of the World Cup. It generated a lot of interest and excitement and to a large extent has enhanced the credibility of the tournament. Yet it was not all smooth and sunny.

On the Thursday after the midweek game against Namibia, one did not know whether to salute or decry their one-point win. It was a niggling, often petulant affair, reminiscent in its ill-tempered undertones of the build-up to the Battle of Harare, the infamous explosion of mindless violence between the Ivorians and Morocco in the 1991 World Cup qualifying rounds.

The fact that the game between the Ivory Coast and Namibia did not degenerate into an all-out battle had more to do with the self-restraint of the Namibians than any Ivorian design or refereeing performance. Had the Namibians been as volatile and bad-tempered as the Moroccans back in 1990, Casablanca 1994 would have entered the history books as another inglorious episode in the Ivory Coast's pursuit of international respectability.

However, their disciplined, almost clinical demolition of Zimbabwe on the Saturday earned them not only a place among the last 16 in South Africa, but also the grudging respect of the pundits. Their controlled performance and their past record suggested that the mayhem the previous Thursday might have been a deliberate ploy, cynically designed and cheerfully implemented to disrupt the Namibians, rather than an accident.

Although the game against Namibia was a shambles, occasionally interrupted by rugby action – most of it of an eminently forgettable quality – the Ivorians, using a combination of legal and illegal means, achieved their aim of upsetting both the rhythm and the organisation of Namibia's supposedly superior outfit. On the credit side, their set-piece play was more than adequate, with a rock-solid scrum and the line-out as the chief operational option. They could kick any ball into touch in the knowledge that their spring-heeled jumpers would retrieve it, regardless who threw it back in.

The possible explanation for the failure in this department of Namibia, who had on the paddock three more than adequate jumpers in Bernard Malgas, Jasper Engelbrecht and Louis van Coller, has more to do with their inflexible thinking and a lack of leadership than with any sensational Ivorian line-out play. The fact that Ivory Coast were vulnerable in the line-out was amply demonstrated by Zimbabwe, who exposed their naivety and lack of experience at the weekend.

But against Namibia, the Ivorians infringed and obstructed, intimidated and bullied. Tight-head prop Touissant Djehi, troublemaker, clown and scrummager emeritus, was the chief culprit. Djehi, who plays for Rodez in France, puffed and huffed, dissented and argued, threatened and occasionally punched. In the Zimbabwe match, warned by both referee Robert Yeman of Wales and coach Dominique Davanier prior to the game, he kept his mouth shut and applied himself to the task, substantially contributing to the Ivorian forward effort and to their highly effective rolling maul in particular.

Ivory Coast put paid to the hopes of Namibia (left) and Zimbabwe (below) to win the African qualifying group in Morocco.

The metamorphosis of Djehi from the villain of the piece to a role-model is the symbol of Ivory Coast's newly found pride and maturity and reflects a superior rugby thinking. The chaos of Thursday and the outstanding discipline on Saturday characterise the opposite ends of the French rugby culture which the Ivorians have absorbed with relish. The two Ivorian coaches, Claude Ezoua, a Bordeaux University graduate, and Dominique Davanier, once a flank forward with Cahors and former

French regional technical director, are by-products of French rugby. The same is true of the Moroccans, who to a man play and live in France. The combined efforts of Ivory Coast and Morocco confronted with the might of Zimbabwe and Namibia mark a significant shift in the balance of power in the African game which has been determined by French expertise and know-how.

The Namibians arrogantly believed that they could win by simply flying the flag, an assumption the Ivorians rudely disagreed with. After their somewhat lucky win against Zimbabwe on the first day, Namibia were foolhardy enough to dismiss the Ivorians as inconsequential – admittedly following Ivory Coast's sub-standard performance in the opening game against Morocco – and decided to use the game to give six of their reserve players a run. They paid dearly for it.

But while Namibia could legitimately claim that they had been taken by surprise by the vigour and the underhand tactics of the Ivory Coast, Zimbabwe had no excuse. They knew what was in store, but even so they seemed ill prepared to handle the lively Ivorians. But whereas the West Africans improved nearly 100 per cent in most areas of their game between Thursday and Saturday, they failed to show any noticeable progress in their goal-kicking, which veered from dreadful to abysmal. Captain Athanse Dali, a recent graduate of Paris University in journalism, is a very clever playmaker and a talented all-rounder. But if he hopes to help his country make an impact in the 1995 World Cup in South Africa he must radically improve his kicking technique.

The Ivorians spent another 80 anxious minutes in the stand as Morocco came tantalisingly close to beating Namibia in the dying seconds of the final game of the tournament. However, the Moroccans, suffering from the same numbing inability to kick, failed to convert pressure into points in their bruising encounter with the Namibians. Had any of the three Moroccan kickers managed to land at least one of the half-dozen penalties given away by Namibia, the Ivorian fairy tale would have come to an abrupt end.

For Morocco, who beat Ivory Coast in the first game of the tournament, the dream scenario involved an Ivorian success in the Zimbabwe game coupled with a Moroccan win against Namibia. In the event, while the Ivorians duly dispatched Zimbabwe, the gallant Moroccans failed to deliver their part of the bargain.

Celebration time for Ivory Coast captain Athanse Dali and coach Dominique Davanier after their narrow win over Namibia.

ALL BLACKS EXCEL IN RUGBY'S MOST EXOTIC EVENT

by BILL McLAREN

There is still nothing to match it in the Rugby Union game. There may be those who do not quite regard the Cathay Pacific-Hongkong Bank seven-a-side tournament as the greatest show on earth, but they must be the ones who have not experienced its particular charisma and magic. The incomparable David Campese has described it as the top tournament of all and it is just that – a marvellous mixture of festival, mardi gras, cultural exchange, keen on-field competition and a general spirit of sportsmanship that pervades the entire tournament as East meets West and North meets South. The fabulous Hong Kong Hilton Hotel, under the genial managership of a splendid Scot, James Smith from Fife, is festooned with rugby players and officials for the week of the tournament, for all 24 squads are based there and it is one of the joyous aspects of the event that players from all over the world rub shoulders and exchange views within its luxurious precincts.

The 1994 tournament, the 19th in the series, proved another memorable affair which had all the ingredients for drama, excitement, thrill and fun and which served up an appetising dish of a final between those Southern Hemisphere giants New Zealand and Australia. With a rich mix of youth and experience responding, like cavalry horses to a bugle, to the inspiring leadership of perhaps the greatest sevens

The impressive new home of the Hong Kong Sevens (above) wascompleted before the 1994 event. The Japanese party (below) enters the spirit of the occasion.

forward of all time, Eric Rush, New Zealand emerged as worthy champions.

Not only did the tournament spawn a torrent of 275 tries, most of the dramatic long-range variety, many of quite dazzling creation, but it was contested against the breathtaking backdrop unique to Hong Kong and in the spectacular new Hong Kong stadium, a green oasis in a sea of concrete which was, incredibly, built in two years and has a capacity of 40,000. Truly a worthy venue for the World Sevens in 1997.

It is, of course, part of the Hong Kong tradition that the minnows, carrying the vociferous support of the vast bulk of the cheery audience, are gobbled up by the sharks. New Zealand swept through Malaysia by 64-0, South Africa beat Thailand 63-0, Western Samoa, the holders, beat Sri Lanka 61-0 and Australia ran up 54 points without reply against Japan. Yet the spirit of the Hong Kong tournament is embodied in the thrill for those less successful nations of taking on the heavyweights of the sevens game and, even in defeat, having the incentive of taking part in one of the three knock-out championships, Cup, Plate and Bowl, on the second day. Thus Sri Lanka, crushed by Western Samoa, still had the satisfaction of reaching the Bowl semi-final by beating Singapore 19-14 in an exciting quarter-final.

Another aspect of the Hong Kong Sevens attraction is that, over the years, the tournament has launched on to the world stage some of the most gifted sevens artists who have then gone on to make a big impact on the fuller version of the game. David Campese, Waisale Serevi, Mesake Rasari and Eric Rush have been typical examples. The latest in the line is an aggressive young man with all the physical attributes of King Kong except that he is quicker! He stands 6 foot 5 inches tall, whistles the scales round to 18 stone 6 pounds, is just out of school and barely 19. The name is Jonah Lomu. He was unknown to the majority of the Hong Kong audience but, by the end, he had emerged as a personality. His skill levels are as high as you would expect of a New Zealand player and his pace and power lent him the appearance of a runaway road-roller. There was a well of sympathy for the inimitable little Serevi when, in the semi-final, he bravely sailed in to sink Lomu and ricocheted off the thundering giant like a bit of flotsam on a raging sea. To his eternal credit Serevi stuck to him like a limpet mine second time around!

Lomu was not the only young unknown to give a hint of future fame. Jim Williams of Australia is a centre with Western Suburbs in Brisbane but, at 6 foot 3 and 15 stone, he made a big impression as a sevens forward with four thrilling tries from deep positions in which his pace was too much even for some of the opposition quickies. There was, too, a lanky New Zealander called Glen Osborne, just 22, whom the Murrayfield crowd might remember scoring four tries and four conversions at the World Sevens in 1993. This time he gorged himself on four tries, 18 conversions and a penalty goal which used up time that Australia needed in the final.

There were hopes among Hong Kong's exiled community that a side from the UK might sweep all before them for the first time since the Barbarians beat Australia by 12-10 in the 1981 final. The President's VII seemed to have the personnel in five members of the England squad which won the 1993 World Sevens – Nick Beal (Northampton), David Scully (Wakefield), Lawrence Dallaglio and Damian Hopley (Wasps) and Chris Sheasby (Harlequins) – two Scottish sevens specialists in Derek Stark (Boroughmuir) and Adam Roxburgh (Kelso), two Fijian forwards, Marika Korovou and Eparama Duvonivono, and Jonathan Sleightholme (Wakefield) who, having taken part in the tens tournament and anticipating a pleasant spectating role for the rest of the weekend, was summoned to the aid of the President's VII. After scoring 11 tries in beating Singapore and a weakened Ireland with Hopley a powerful force, the President's VII took the lead against the holders, Western Samoa, with a try by Stark after a typical tackle-bursting surge by Dallaglio. Sheasby's street wisdom brought another try to lift hopes at 12-14, but chances to put the issue beyond doubt were not brought to fruition. Western Samoa's Brian Lima, who had nine tries in the World Sevens, recorded his seventh in just three ties to seal the President's VII's fate at 21-12.

Ireland were handicapped by the absence of two experienced quick men, Richard Wallace (Garryowen) and Nial Woods (Blackrock), and by the injury that removed Eric Elwood after nine minutes of the opening tie against Singapore. Despite the impressive work-rate of Denis McBride (Malone), Ireland lost by 12-14 in the Plate quarter-final to the Americans, who then shared in an enthralling final. Although they led 7-0 and 14-7 their opponents, the Koreans, fizzed about the paddock like tsetse flies and were the eventual worthy Plate winners by 26-21, having also eliminated Canada and Tonga, who were not the same force without Isu Tuivai.

David Campese captained the Australian team into the final on his farewell visit to Hong Kong, but New Zealand spoiled Campo's party with an emphatic win.

Taipei defenders swarm around Australia's Ilie Tabua on the opening day of the tournament.

Scotland blew cold, hot, then cold again. They barely got off first base as they were hustled out of any rhythm by Hong Kong, whose first try in victory by 15-5 was by Vaughan Going, nephew of the famous All Black scrum-half, Sid Going. Argentina then beat Hong Kong by 26-5, whereupon the Scots put the cat among the pigeons with some cracking interplay for tries by Michael Dods of Gala, Scott Nichol (Selkirk) and Cameron Little (Glasgow High/Kelvinside) in a 24-14 win over Argentina. As all three in the pool had the same number of pool points, Argentina qualified for the Cup with six tries, Scotland for the Plate with five and Hong Kong for the Bowl with four.

In the Plate quarter-final Scotland lost Craig Joiner (Melrose) early with cartilage damage and, despite the valiant efforts of Dods and Nichol, they just could not cope with the electrifying pace and ball transference of the Japanese, for whom the Fijian Lovokuro Sirilo scored important tries. Winners by 26-12, Japan then were denied enough ball by the Americans, who beat them 29-7 in the Plate semi-final.

Hong Kong continued to keep the crowd at a fever pitch of excitement, however, when they responded to the stern coaching of their guru, George Simpkin of Waikato, and the captaincy of their American schoolmaster personality, Stuart Krohn, by winning the Bowl Championship with a 24-12 margin over Portugal, who were making their first appearance at the Hong Kong event. Portugal produced a crowd favourite in Pedro Murinello, who scampered miles for six splendid tries, two of them in the tight 10-7 defeat of Romania in the Bowl semi-final.

The big guns contested the Cup quarter-finals with a blaze of mesmeric ball-handling and marvellous running. Australia achieved the only walkover – 43-0 over Argentina – but France brought the house down with two late tries from Francois Preux (Pau) and Marc Lievremont (Perpignan) before going down 12-21 to New Zealand. Lovely tries by Chester Williams and Joost van der Westhuizen gave South Africa a 12-7 lead over Fiji, but a touch of Serevi magic set up a late try for Sakeasi Vonolagi and Serevi's conversion took Fiji through by 14-12.

In his ninth Hong Kong tournament, the burly Lolani Koko gave Western Samoa a flying start with a try in the first 30 seconds of the top semi-final against Australia, but Jim Williams scorched 70 metres for his score and the ebb and flow brought the first and only spell of extra time at 17-17. When Junior Paramor was penalised for not staying on his feet Campese potted the winning penalty goal and the holders were out. New Zealand led Fiji by 21-0 after only five minutes of the other semi-final but Fiji got back to 21-14 before a fascinating sequence of 12 passes, long and short, most of them improvised, spawned the cushion New Zealand try by Rush.

In the final, New Zealand won more ball and made it work in brilliant fashion so that when the human bulldozer, Lomu, scored his try soon after the break New Zealand led 29-6. Tries by Williams (his second), the indefatigable David Wilson and the new scrum-half find, George Gregan, gave Australia some respectability but as Campese admitted after the tie: 'They were the better side on the day. They won more ball and used it effectively.'

In five ties the New Zealanders scored 183 points, including 28 tries. They had the ideal amalgam of ball-winners and ball-manipulators, their support running was intuitively brilliant and virtually every one of their squad was capable of scoring a long-range try.

Although the pitch was a bit short of grass in patches, partly because of the amount of building work on the super new stadium, the tournament proved another huge success. The weather was kind and the good-natured audience reacted in distinctive fashion to the Grand Parade of teams and of the referees with their dark glasses and white sticks, the artistry and elegance of the girls from the Sacred Heart Canossian College in their colourful display of oriental culture, the Song of the Sunflower, and the

Farewell from the finalists at the end of another memorable weekend.

magical fare provided by the 24 competing nations. It is to be hoped that England will be able to adjust their schedules in order to send a fully representative national VII to the tournament next time. That is no more than this great event deserves. Meanwhile, players and officials can barely wait for the 20th Cathay Pacific-Hongkong Bank tournament to come along next March and April. The simple fact is that there is nothing quite like the Hong Kong Sevens in the entire world of Rugby Union.

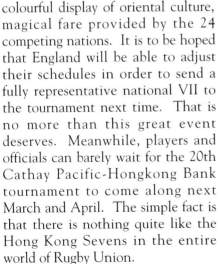

FRANCOIS PIENAAR – SOUTH AFRICA'S 'BIONIC MAN'

by CHRIS THAU

The frustration of the South African rugby constituency at the inability of the once invincible Springboks to return to the top of the ladder has reached a boiling-point. Occasional fiasco has been treated with disdain in South Africa. Consistent failure brings the worst out of the South African rugby supporter, led and willing to believe that the Springboks deserve to rule the roost.

The intensity of the current campaign reflects the frustration of the South Africans, who are unable to come to terms with their country's halting return to international respectability. The man who takes most of the flak is Jakobus François Pienaar, a 27-year-old law student and businessman, the captain of the Springboks. Having to put up with unprecedented levels of public and media criticism is nowadays part of the Springbok captain's brief.

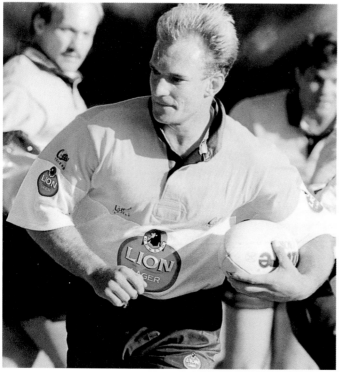

François Pienaar in training with the South African squad for the Test matches against England.

Pienaar explains: 'One of the most difficult aspects of captaincy in a Springbok situation as opposed to, say, Transvaal, is the extreme demands of the public. This pressure is overwhelming, and I have to admit that there are moments when I feel that no matter what I do, I cannot win. There is this obsessive expectation of success. And if it does not come, then a scapegoat must be found immediately. They need to find someone who they could crucify.

'What makes rugby such a fascinating sport, though, is that you can play well and still lose. I have no problem with that. Losing is part of rugby, as much as winning is. The two co-exist, like the good and the bad, the beautiful and the ugly. They are the opposite ends of the playing spectrum. It is about the way one handles defeat and success. Humility in winning is as important as dignity in defeat. If you have a game plan and apply it flawlessly, every player in the side plays to the best of his ability, and you still lose, then I have no problem with the defeat. This is the message we have been trying to put across to our public: look for quality rather than wins. Winning will come as part of a better game.'

Before his international debut against France in 1993, Pienaar made an impassioned appeal to the media, asking the journalists to help South African rugby rid itself of the provincialism entrenched by isolation and the elevation of the Currie Cup to a near-holy status. The example of the unhappy tour to France in 1992, when the tour party cracked along provincial lines as the defeats piled up, is still vivid in memories. Pienaar claims that the experience of the Transvaal side he captains could be used as an example to overcome the legacy of the isolation.

'I believe in the value of the group as therapy. My philosophy in the Transvaal team is that we talk to each other rather than about each other. It is vital to communicate, and in this respect I am the facilitator. On a tour things could easily go wrong once you start losing, and you have guys who have failed to make the side. Players tend to become negative and frustrated. It is the role of the captain to defuse the approaching crisis, let the players get their frustration off their chests. Dialogue and communication are part of man-management and they are the only way to mould a group of individuals into a collective.'

Pienaar, an articulate leader with an astute rugby brain, is embarked on an uphill battle to prove his worth both as a player and as a captain. His personal performance in the games of the recently concluded tour to New Zealand can hardly be faulted. His commitment is legendary and his Transvaal coach, Kitch Christie, has been trying to convince him not to play each game as if it were his last. Bob Dwyer rates the abrasive Pienaar as one of the most effective open-side flankers in the game while the critical New Zealanders have accepted him as a player with a great potential.

However, being recognised in foreign lands does not automatically qualify him for a prophet status in his own country. The criticism of him is not particularly focused. It is rather diffuse, a combination of rumours, hearsay and gossip. The most damaging allegation is that he is injury-prone. His concussion in the Wellington game and his subsequent decision to wear headgear have fuelled the debate. His critics, in what is arguably the most intense rugby landscape in the world, say that the injury record of the youthful Transvaal captain could be a liability for a tough, long-term campaign like the World Cup. There is very little Pienaar can do to deflect such criticism.

Four years ago Pienaar suffered a horrific ankle injury. He broke his ankle, the bones split and pierced the skin. But South Africa has excellent orthopaedic surgeons and two months later he was back in training. Three years ago, he was punched from behind at a line-out and had his jaw broken in two. He was carried off holding his collapsed mandible, like Graham Price of Wales in the infamous Test against Australia, and he needed a platinum plaque and screws inserted to keep it in place.

'This injury affected my self-confidence badly. I was out of the game for a long time and when I recommenced I kept looking behind, expecting a blow, but eventually I managed to overcome the psychological trauma and carry on. In 1992, as I started to get back in stride, I collided with one of my colleagues during training and tore the ligaments in my knee.'

Pienaar was concussed while making a head-on tackle on Wellington winger Alaska Taufa in the third game of the New Zealand tour. Inspired by the epic win against England, when he silenced his critics with a stirring performance, Pienaar played like a man possessed. By the Wellington game he was probably playing the best rugby of his career. Not surprisingly, he forgot the advice of his coach, Kitch Christie, to avoid the crash-tackling, a habit which had become his trademark. The concussion in Wellington was the second knock-out this season, and the fourth of his career. The previous concussion took place at the beginning of the season during a game in the M-Net series, when he got a bump to the head during one of his reckless tackles. A full medical examination and a brain scan revealed no damage and he was cleared by the doctors to resume playing.

Long before the emergence of Pienaar, one of the most gifted centre threequarters the game has ever seen, Wallaby John Brass had to overcome a similar reputation for fragility before becoming an established international. Eventually, Brass crossed the Rubicon to Rugby League and became a dual international, one of the very few to have enjoyed ultimate success in both codes. However, his durability was questioned time and again. The examples are abundant. Scotland's Chris Rea emerged from a horrific series of injuries to establish himself as one of the most talented centres of his time. France's Laurent Cabannes, dubbed the 'Bionic Man' for the countless operations he has suffered, has returned to full fitness after a year in the wilderness. Pienaar's second lay-off with concussion was after last year's Currie Cup final against Natal. He recalls the incident:

'It was one of the most intense, physically demanding games I have ever played in. I had never experienced such intensity in our games overseas. Very often the fine dividing line between physical and brutal was crossed during that game. In the second half I was tackling blindly. I was not focused enough and I hit a knee as I went into a tackle. I went off concussed.

'The previous concussion happened long time ago, though, in 1988, or '89. I was knocked unconscious during a game against Western Province. I swallowed my tongue and I was told afterwards that I had something that looked like an epileptic fit. I woke up in the ambulance about half an hour later. I was told by the doctors not to play for a while, but I was back at it after three weeks. With hindsight it might have been wiser to take a longer break. But this is the way we are made. I am passionate about my game, I would play anywhere, any time. Even now, if I had a small injury, a wrist or a rib, I would probably hide it, such is the desire to perform. We are possessed by rugby. It is more than a religion in South Africa, it is the soul of the nation.'

François Pienaar in possession against England during the second Test in Cape Town, closely attended by Will Carling, Rob Andrew and Phil de Glanville.

IS THE WORLD CUP WORTH IT?

by JOHN REASON
Rugby Correspondent of the Sunday Telegraph

Once every 100 years, the amateur game of Rugby Union football finds itself looking straight down the barrel of professionalism. It did so in 1894. It is doing so again in 1994.

The tours that England and Ireland have recently made of South Africa and Australia have left neither the committee of the Rugby Union nor the committee of the Irish Rugby Union in any doubt that sooner or later they will have to face just as stark a choice as England faced 100 years ago when their great northern clubs broke away to form the Rugby League. They will not make that choice this side of the 1995 Rugby World Cup. Their loyalty to South Africa is too deep-rooted to upset it. But when that tournament is over, England and Ireland, and maybe various other countries, will have to decide whether to compete in any World Cup which may be organised in future.

As Ian Beer, the outgoing president of the Rugby Union, has sadly and gravely remarked, they will also have to decide whether to continue to play international matches against South Africa and Australia. South Africa are now in much the same position as France were in the 1930s. Then, the French were excommunicated from international amateur rugby because of the rampant professionalism in their club game. Unfortunately, the years of South Africa's isolation from the world of sport have led to a dog-eat-dog situation in their country. The leading provinces bid for the best players, and did it with such determination that the game inevitably became professional at the top level.

The Australians saw this at once when they returned to play South Africa in 1992, and, rubbing their hands with relish, they are scrambling down the same road just as fast as they can. Australia have always been obsessed with the threat of Rugby League in their own country. That threat has always been there, and Australia have always found highly talented players to fill the gaps left by the depredations of League, but the Union game has always seen itself as the underdog and almost powerless in opposition to Rugby League. Now all that has changed. Australia's success in the 1991 World Cup brought such international acclaim and such an enhanced status at home that they have persuaded themselves they are ready to take on Rugby League as a fully professional game. They shrug and wave aside the profound reservations of a vastly more experienced man like Ireland's Syd Millar as the vapourings of an irrelevant. We will see.

Dr Danie Craven, who bestrode the world of rugby like a colossus for the last 20 years of his life, saw all this coming. Five years ago he told me that the most disturbing consequence of the isolation of rugby in South Africa had been the slide into professionalism of the six major provincial unions in South Africa. Those are the ones with Test match grounds. He said: 'Because we have no international competition to provide a balance, our provincial Currie Cup competition has become so important in terms of its appeal to South Africa's rugby public that our six Test unions bid against each other to sign up the best players from the smaller unions. They are all professional now, and some of them do not care who knows.

'It is as if they have become six separate countries. They are like fortresses looking out on a hostile world. Six separate laagers. I am sure this has happened because we have no international rugby identity at the moment.'

Craven then told me that he was seriously thinking of professionalising all six of those unions: Western Province, Eastern Province, Natal, Orange Free State, Transvaal and Northern Transvaal. He would then let them go on playing each other, week in and week out, until they died either of boredom or incest. He said that South Africa would continue its membership of the International Rugby Football Board because, like the Pied Piper of Hamlin, he would gather all his country's small unions and lead them into the paths of righteousness. 'Our international status would be very much reduced, but at least we would still be amateur,' he said.

The effect on South African rugby would have been just as significant as the breakaway of England's northern clubs in the 1890s. But by then, Danie Craven was becoming increasingly involved in trying to bridge the racial and political divide in South Africa, and that was a much greater work. As Nelson Mandela has said, Danie Craven was the man who effectively started the whole process of racial reconciliation, and that was a much bigger and a much more important war than a domestic battle over professionalism in South African rugby. But England's tour of South Africa has left the Rugby Union committee in no doubt that the battle about professionalism has to be fought all over again, just as it was in 1894.

Hugo Porta, perhaps Argentina's greatest player, and now his country's ambassador in South Africa, is of exactly the same opinion. His concern is not about professionalism in South African rugby, but about

Two Argentinians who chose to play under a new flag: Enrique Rodriguez in Australian colours (above) and Diego Dominguez (above right) representing Italy.

professionalism in the game worldwide. 'More than 100 of Argentina's best players are now playing in Italy and France,' he said. 'They are making a lot of money. Some of them are even playing for Italy.

'I know that New Zealanders and Australians and South Africans are playing in Italy, and have done for years, and I know that those countries go on choosing those players to play in international tournaments like the World Cup and the Hong Kong Sevens. Argentina will not do that. They will stay amateur. But that means that we cannot compete. We go to Hong Kong: we make friends, we do a bit of shopping. But we lose.

'It's the same in the World Cup. We are just about good enough to qualify at the bottom end of the tournament, but all we can do is make up the numbers. We have no hope of winning, or of representing the true strength of Argentina's rugby.'

Hugo Porta is absolutely right. If New Zealand, Australia and South Africa were stripped of their best 100 players, they would be just as hard pressed as Argentina, possibly even more so. But no one is in any doubt that the world of rugby is being divided into haves and have-nots, and especially, it is being divided into players who are haves and have-nots in financial terms.

There is equally no doubt that the main architect of this division has been the Rugby World Cup, because it has put so much added pressure on players in terms of training and commitment that it has made them virtually unemployable, except as rugby players. So, in about one year's time, we will have to ask ourselves whether the World Cup is worth it.

Will Carling enjoys a dip in the Indian Ocean during England's tour of South Africa.

Will Carling,
Steve Ojomoh,
Paul Hull and
Damian Hopley
battle for
possession in
England's 26-24
win over Western
Transvaal.

A relaxing break
for the England
squad on safari
north of Durban.

Rory Underwood
with some young
rugby enthusiasts
during a visit to
Soshenguve
township.

THE HEART OF ASIA

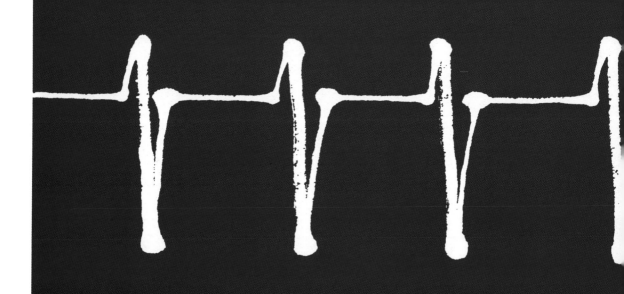

We serve the most dynamic part of the world with over 650 fligh

CATHAY PACIFIC

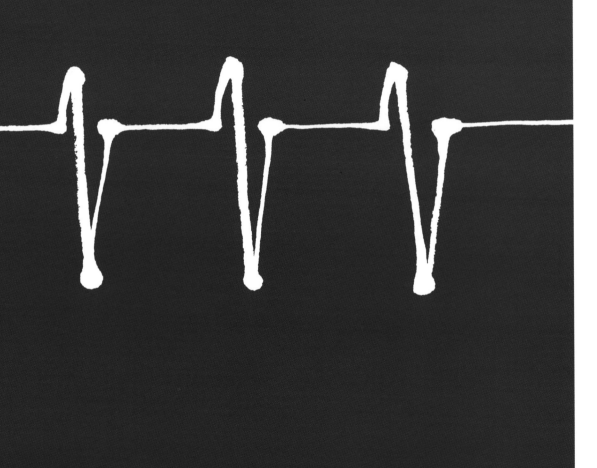

eek to and from Hong Kong. Cathay Pacific. The Heart of Asia.

Matt Poole
demonstrates to
young South
Africans how to
overcome a
height difference
in the line-out!

Papua New Guinea disclose their secret weapon at the Hong Kong Sevens.

Morocco, the host
nation for the
African qualifying
tournament, just
missed a place in
the finals in
South Africa.
They beat
eventual qualifiers
Ivory Coast on
the field but lost
to them on points
difference in the
final league table.

Headed for the World Cup in South Africa – Ble Aka (left) and Ernest Bley, two members of the powerful Ivory Coast team that won the African qualifying competition in Morocco.

The top players have a number of things in common.

Experience of playing conditions around the world. A capacity to read the game. A sense of teamwork. Strength. Speed. And, above all, the ability to make fast decisions.

HongkongBank
The Hongkong and Shanghai Banking Corporation Limited

Fast decisions. Worldwide.

THE DEATH OF THE MINNOW

by CHRIS THAU

It is to be hoped the derogatory label 'minnow' will be dropped from the rugby vocabulary. And this is not because suddenly arrogance is in short supply. No, its demise has been forced upon the rugby community because the term has become obsolete. Who could be described as the minnows of the 1995 World Cup?

Italy, until recently regarded as the nearly men of international rugby, came within three points of beating the reigning world champions, Australia – and this was not a fluke. Western Samoa rattled Five Nations champions Wales, and if allowed to retain their current playing personnel until the World Cup they could trouble anybody. Tonga have just replaced Western Samoa in the Super-10 competition and by May 1995 they could be in lethal form. Canada have already graduated as one of the giant-killers of the international circuit, while Argentina and Romania have given samples of their prowess and capacity to upset the favourites on a number of occasions. The minnow has become an obsolete term, expelled from the language by the Rugby World Cup 'meritocratic' hierarchy.

Until July 1994, Italy beating Australia sounded like fiction of dubious quality. However, the impossible nearly happened in the First Test in Brisbane, when a combination of Italian naivety and Australian luck prevented the world of rugby from being turned on its head. The Italians proved their mettle again a week later in Melbourne, when the difference was one of Campese's referee-made tries.

The Italians have been building up their strength in depth, quietly and unobtrusively, for some time. They aim to make a significant impact in the 1995 World Cup in South Africa. The tournament has concentrated the minds of the Latins beautifully and their evolution from sorrowful victims of All Black menace in 1987 to merciless torturers of the Czech Republic in

Argentinian German Llanes wins line-out possession in the South American World Cup qualifying match against Chile.

Italian coach
Georges Coste
(right) plans the
match ahead
with Franco
Properzi-Curti
(left) and Massimo
Cuttitta (centre).

1994 is a symbol both of their ambition and of the suction effect of the William Webb Ellis tournament. The initially unheralded arrival of new coach Georges Coste has provided the Italian team with a catalyst.

Italy is now one of the powers to be reckoned with and whoever takes them for granted does so at his own peril. Mind you the time has come for Italy to decline the dubious privilege of playing in the so-called non-cap internationals. The unofficial international used to be a symbol of the arrogance of the powerful. Today it is a convenient smokescreen to hide the fear of defeat.

Unquestionably, the World Cup has given the game a much-needed boost. Throughout the world, coaching, playing and refereeing standards have risen, fitness levels have improved and the status of the game has been enhanced. Until ten years ago, players and administrators from the so-called developing countries were complaining that, for their nations, there was no light at the end of the tunnel.

There was no system in place to motivate a young man from Dallas, USA or Montevideo, Uruguay, or Abidjan, Ivory Coast to concentrate on the skills of rugby football in the hope that one day he could top the world's hierarchy. There was no system in place to create role-models in countries where rugby football lived an almost secret existence. There was no system to inform the youngsters about the joy and the values of the game. Rugby World Cup has changed all that. It has provided the game with a global shop window in which the image, the status and the heroes are on display at a time when rugby is undergoing a massive reappraisal of its place and position in the world and in society.

It is no coincidence that the first World Cup, an experimental affair with 16 invited nations, was held a year after the IRFB decided to go international. Historically, the game has retained its ethos and traditions because, though played in most countries, it never really took the world by storm. Playing-wise, bar a couple of exceptional cases like New Zealand and South Africa, Rugby Union has remained a minority game, enjoying a limited appeal mostly among middle and upper classes. It is true that it is filling the stadia in the Five Nations capitals, but this is a comparatively recent phenomenon and, anyway, a large percentage of those who pay substantial sums for a hospitality package at Twickenham or Parc des Princes have very little interest in the game.

The decision of the IRFB to take over the world of rugby, forced upon the governing body by developments elsewhere and by the threat of a professional circus, has led to the birth of the World Cup. Like everything else in the game it started as a cosy affair designed for the big boys and using the minnows as a supporting cast. Fiji's heroically absurd challenge against France in the 1987 quarter-finals could not really be labelled an upset, though it had nearly given the septuagenarian FFR Committee watching the game a collective heart-attack.

The 1991 tournament brought about subtle changes. The general public observed that the big boys, with the exception of Wales, remained unscathed. However, the connoisseur will have noticed that Italy, at the wrong end of a 70-6 drubbing at the hands of New Zealand in 1991,

Costica Cojocariu wins the line-out for Romania against Russia in their World Cup qualifying match.

gave the All Blacks serious headaches this time round; that the USA, though defeated, improved beyond recognition; that Canada, applauded in 1987 for their bravery, were matching the best in every department in 1991. Western Samoa, who missed the 1987 World Cup due to insufficient information about their playing prowess, reached the quarter-finals, establishing themselves in due course as the undisputed social climbers of international rugby. But all these signs were for the eye of the expert. By and large, the earth-shattering results failed to arrive.

The year 1995 could be the one in which the established order of the game is challenged. The Italians have nothing to lose but their inhibitions. The same is true of the other minnows. The World Cup is the ladder by which the more ambitious can reach the top. The momentum generated by the world event is gathering pace. The days when the 'big eight' – the so-called founding members of the IRFB Council – could live happily in the knowledge that their position and privileges were secure are gone.

However, the development in the world has been uneven, commensurate with the ambitions and more significantly the resources available. As a consequence the gap between the playing standards of the wealthy and those of the poor has widened. While it has provided the smaller nations with a canvas on which to express their aspirations, the World Cup has not offered them the equivalent means to fulfil them. And this is the next priority of the governing body, the IRFB. The strategic plan devised by secretary Keith Rowlands and former All Black captain Bob Stuart lists development as one of the major priorities facing the game.

Yet levelling the playing fields could prove the most difficult task facing the administrators. The games in the Central European qualifying zone prove the point. The Czechs, who suffered a Rugby World Cup record thrashing at the hands of Italy, were more than competitive 17 years ago when they lost 10-4 to the same opposition in Prague. The Dutch nearly beat Italy in the qualifying rounds in 1990. In 1994 the Italians annihilated them.

Both Italy and the Netherlands made progress compared to 1990, but the gap between the two has actually increased. The difference has nothing to do with raw talent or commitment. In terms of guts and sheer pride the Dutch have nothing to learn from anybody. In fact, the split reflects the disparity in resources available to the game. And of those resources, time is the most significant. Former Scotland captain Peter Kininmonth, a millionaire businessman in the City of London, once said: 'Being professional has nothing to do with being paid for playing. It is about the time one puts into the game.' Italian players benefit from vastly superior resources and have far more time to train than their Dutch counterparts. If this is indeed the yardstick, while most Italians are full-time or part-time professionals, the Dutch are pure amateurs. This is not a moral dichotomy. It is a fact of life and must be addressed as such, as the retiring Dutch captain Johan de Vries observed.

Korea, winners of the Plate at the 1994 Hong Kong Sevens, are among those teams contesting the final place in the World Cup through the Asian qualifying competition.

THE WORLD ORDER

by IAN ROBERTSON

Arguably, the most significant international in the first nine months of 1994 was the one-off Bledisloe Cup match in Sydney in August. It featured the winners of the 1987 World Cup, New Zealand against the winners of the 1991 World Cup, Australia, to determine the probable pecking order for the 1995.

As befitted the clash between the top two rugby sides in the world in the 1990s, the capacity crowd of 42,000 witnessed a magnificent game of rugby. For those of us in Britain who had had to endure a very moderate Five Nations Championship, the scintillating and explosive performance by the Wallabies and All Blacks provided a sharp and painful reminder that there is still a considerable gulf between the Northern and Southern Hemisphere sides.

Australia played some breathtaking rugby in the first half to storm to a commanding lead of 17-6. The forwards produced a devastating display of power and control which severely dented All Black pride, but which would have totally destroyed any of the four Home Unions.

Australia have the best tight five forwards in world rugby at the moment and it is very hard to imagine how the Home Unions will be able to cope with a front row of Daly, Kearns and McKenzie or two line-out jumpers of the size and expertise of Eales and Morgan. Behind this formidable platform they have the dynamism of Willie Ofahengaue, the tactical discipline of Gavin and the footballing skill of Wilson.

By the time Lynagh and Horan return to the back division the Wallabies will boast as much strike power as any team at the World Cup. They have rounded off their best-ever season with a remarkable 100 per cent record and, best of all, they have unearthed a fantastic prospect at scrum-half in George Gregan.

In the second half of the Bledisloe Cup match, Australia had to do a great deal of defending and covering which they did brilliantly and this mighty impressive rearguard action was highlighted by the tackle of the year when Gregan saved a try with a thumping tackle on All Black wing Wilson. It is very hard to score against Australia. They remain the best team in the world.

New Zealand have had a nightmare 12 months. They lost to England at Twickenham in November 1993 and lost both Tests against France in the summer of 1994 as well as the Bledisloe Cup to Australia.

However, in the second half of that epic match, they staged a dramatic recovery and came within an ace of winning the game with a last-gasp try. We saw typical, traditional, driving New Zealand forward play of the highest class and plenty of thrilling, running back play. If they could reproduce those 40 minutes of rugby right through the World Cup they would be unstoppable. On the other hand, if they play the way they did against England and France they will be in for another disappointing tournament just as they experienced in 1991.

Potentially, Australia and New Zealand are the best two countries in the world and I expect them to meet in the 1995 final.

Third in the pecking order on recent results would have to be France, who have finally got their act together after two seasons of experimenting. Locked together as joint fourth in the rankings come England and South Africa. After all, they did share the Test series in Pretoria and Cape Town, with one decisive win each. With home advantage in 1995, South Africa would just have the edge over England.

Wales, despite having to pre-qualify for the World Cup, won the Five Nations title in 1994 and deserve to be rated sixth best with Scotland. Ireland, Western Samoa and Canada are right behind. But whatever happens in the Northern Hemisphere in the Home Championship in the first three months of 1995, I guarantee that Australia will go into the 1995 World Cup as favourites hotly pursued by New Zealand. If these two sides do indeed meet in the final in Johannesburg and produce a game of similar intensity, passion, brilliance and excitement to the one which thrilled the rugby world in August 1994, we are in for an unforgettable treat.

On the Home Front

ENGLAND ARE WORLD CHAMPIONS

by ALAN LORIMER

Women's rugby may have been the butt of masculine humour in the past but such manifest expressions of male chauvinism must now be consigned to the pages of history. Rugby for women is here to stay and moreover it looks set to attract a large number of new female adherents to a game already acknowledged as the fastest-growing sport. Last April women's rugby celebrated its maturity by staging the second World Championship event and in doing so proved beyond doubt that an enormous amount of progress has been made since the 1991 World Cup in Wales.

Eleven countries – exactly 50 per cent of the nations currently playing women's rugby – were represented in Scotland in a championship that had been arranged in just under three months. Scotland became the host of the World Championships only after arrangements to hold the event in Holland came unstuck. It said much for the fledgling Women's Union in Scotland that they were able to organise the tournament in such a short time, albeit with administrative help from the Scottish Rugby Union.

Ireland beat Japan in their play-off for third place in the Shield competition in the Women's World Championships.

It was hardly surprising, given what happened in the early matches of the 1991 men's World Cup, not to mention the lack of qualifying matches, that cricket scores resulted in the pool games, notably in favour of the USA, who notched up an aggregate of 232 points in their two matches, against Sweden and Japan. In fact it was Pool D which turned out to be the most competitive. Wales and Canada both defeated Kazakhstan but in the crunch match Wales beat Canada 11-5 to win the pool.

Galashiels and Melrose were the venues for the quarter-finals. The

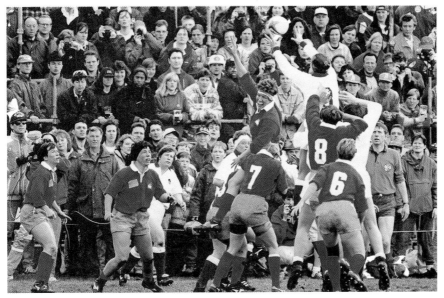

Good line-out possession for England in the World Cup final against the United States.

USA, encouraged by an entourage of travelling supporters, maintained their high scoring rate with a 76-0 victory over Ireland. In contrast England, runners-up in Wales three years ago, made a meal of things before overcoming Canada 24-10 to book a place in the semi-final.

At the Greenyards France just failed to hit a century with a 99-0 win over Japan, but again the other quarter-final, between Scotland and Wales, proved to be of an entirely different nature. In a competitive match it was the combined experience of Bess Evans at scrum-half and Lisa Burgess at number 8, complemented by the flair of Kate Richards at full-back and the finishing of winger Kim Yau, that won the game for the Welsh.

It was to be the end of the road for Wales, who were overrun 56-15 by the USA in the first of the semi-finals at Netherdale, a match memorable for the five-try contribution from the exciting American full-back Jen Crawford. So there was a place in the final for the USA – but would they meet France or England? Gallic flair has not yet extended to the women's game in France and thus it was the more efficient England team which claimed the other place in the final with an 18-6 win.

The host country, Scotland, having defeated Ireland 10-3 to reach the final of the Shield, gave the women's game north of the border an enormous boost by beating Canada at Meggetland. Metropolitan Police officer Elaine Black, originally from Fort William, kicked two vital penalties but the crunch try for the Scots came from another Highlander, Jeni Sheerin from Inverness.

One wonders what those who watched the first international between Scotland and England back in 1871 at Raeburn Place would have made of a women's international rugby game being played over a century later on the same ground. What is certain is that the women's final between the USA and England attracted a far bigger crowd than the 1871 event.

England team manager Val Moore had predicted that the final would be a 'clash of styles'. But on the day which approach would prove to be the more effective? Few had expected such a decisive answer. England simply scrummaged their opponents out of the game, winning two penalty try awards from attempted pushover scores and a third try from an actual pushover. Without a regular supply of possession, the USA could not use their talented back line as they had hoped, although on meagre rations they did engineer four superb tries, two by Jen Crawford and one apiece for Elise Huffer and Patty Jervey. An interception try by Jacqui Edwards and a well-constructed score by Jane Mitchell, together with an all-round display of kicking skills by captain Karen Almond, gave England victory by 38-23.

The England women's team had, it seems, learned that winning might not be about playing attractive rugby, and in that respect they may be emulating the men's team just a little too closely for the good of the game. England have perhaps set the forward standards for the next World Championship in 1908. If the women's game continues to make the same progress then the next women's world tournament promises to be an even better event.

World champions: the victorious England squad after the final.

FOUR PLAYER PROFILES

Karen Almond

One of the outstanding players of the 1991 World Cup, Karen Almond enjoyed another wonderful tournament in 1994, when she captained England to victory in the final against the Cup-holders, the USA.

'We learned a great deal from 1991, when we played the same style right through the competition and realised after it was all over that we should have been prepared to adopt different tactics against different opponents.'

England deliberately ensured that all 26 members of their squad for the second World Cup played at least once, and most of them twice, in the pool matches. This had the double advantage of giving everyone big-match experience and allowing some of the top players a rest.

'The best atmosphere was at Raeburn Place in Edinburgh, where we had a good win over Scotland. We then improved on our 12-8 win over Canada in Toronto by beating them 24-10 in the quarter-finals. After beating France 18-6 in the semi-final we watched videos of how the Welsh forwards scored three tries against America in their semi-final. Having played running rugby earlier in the tournament, we decided we could beat America in a forward battle and with this different emphasis in our tactical approach we beat them 38-23. This victory was unquestionably the highlight of my whole rugby career.'

Along with all the other players, Karen praised Scotland for organising the tournament so efficiently at such short notice and making it such a fantastic and memorable occasion.

Debbie Francis

After first playing rugby as a student at Leeds University nine years ago, Debbie played club rugby at Finchley and then for the past few seasons at Richmond. A strong, aggressive and multi-talented left wing, she is in a unique situation to compare the first two Women's World Cups because she was one of the real stars of the England side which reached the final in 1991 and in 1994 she helped Scotland win the Shield.

'The standard overall was not so high in 1994 because several of the good sides were missing – notably New Zealand, Holland, Italy and Spain. But the standard of the top two or three sides had improved enormously.

The English had made great strides forward and they dominated the second World Cup. Their pack really outplayed America in the final but I thought the American backs were tremendous. They all took the ball flat out at real pace and produced some wonderful running rugby. All the other countries will now try to build a pack as good as England's and a back division as good as America's for the next World Championships. America and Canada both have very good sides but suffer because they can't play enough games of international rugby; they are geographically isolated.

'I have found both World Cups equally exciting for different reasons. In 1991 it was a thrill because it was the first, it was organised by four of my fellow Richmond-based players and because we reached the final. In 1994, I was delighted that Scotland, as a relatively new international side, managed to win the Shield by beating Canada. Roll on the next one.'

Pogo Paterson

Even though Scotland finished only fifth best in the 1994 World Championships, in winning the Shield final, their young side showed dramatic improvement in the relatively short time they have competed as

an international team. They produced one outstanding player in Pogo Paterson, who would certainly have been good enough to win selection in any composite side picked from the 12 competing countries. A tremendous all-round talent, she was so aggressive in defence that in three consecutive matches she tackled her opponents so hard that not one of the three finished the game. At almost 6 foot and 11 stone, she was quite a handful in attack and made some of the best breaks in the whole of the World Championships.

'The thing that pleased me most has been the way the team has kept improving from my very first cap, when we lost to Wales 23-0 in December 1993, to losing only 8-0 to the same Welsh side in the World Championship quarter-final, to actually beating Canada in the final of the Shield. That match was my main highlight of the World Championships, especially as I helped to make the winning try, which Jeni Sheerin scored. I also thought our opening game against England was a fantastic experience, even though we lost. The atmosphere was incredible, with 5,000 people packed round the ground. The whole tournament was played with great spirit and the social side was terrific. Around 300 players took part and no matter what the results, everyone had an unforgettable time.'

Tara Flanagan

The gloriously amateur nature of women's rugby was clearly underlined by the huge sacrifices so many of the participants had to make just to be in Scotland for the World Championships. The gold medal goes to Tara Flanagan. This enthusiastic fanatic had the shattering experience of returning home in January 1994 to find the earthquake in California in the act of reducing her apartment near Los Angeles to rubble. She side-stepped past policemen and firemen, despite their protestations, to sprint into her apartment and emerge in double-quick time clutching her rugby boots and the medal she received when America won the 1991 World Cup.

'Winning that World Cup medal was the biggest highlight of my sporting career and I was not prepared to let it disappear forever in an earthquake. My biggest disappointment in rugby was losing the 1994 World Championship final because we were outplayed up front. We knew our back division was capable of winning the match if they had a decent share of possession but we had not anticipated the power play of the English pack.

'We will be much better prepared next time, but the really frustrating thing is that we may have to wait for years until the next World Championship before we meet again. There's no doubt the European countries are fortunate that so many play international rugby. There are the four Home Union sides plus another ten on mainland Europe. We can play Canada and that's about it. Having said that, I would not have missed the 1994 World Championship for anything and I am already looking forward to the next one.'

MAXIMISING ENGLAND'S TALENTS

by JACK ROWELL, England Manager
Interviewed by IAN ROBERTSON

England won only three of their eight matches on the tour of South Africa but they played superbly to win the First Test and the whole squad gained a great deal of valuable experience in readiness for the 1995 World Cup. As part of their preparation England played at all three grounds where they will be most likely to be playing in the World Cup: King's Park in Durban, Newlands in Cape Town and Ellis Park in Johannesburg.

Fortunately for England, the man masterminding their World Cup plan is their manager, Jack Rowell. They could not be in better hands. Indeed, major English sport at the moment is being led by three outstanding men of vision: Jack Rowell in rugby, Terry Venables in soccer and Ray Illingworth in cricket.

Rowell was a successful player and coach at Gosforth before joining Bath as coach in 1977. In his last ten years as coach he guided Bath to four League Championships and eight Cup victories at Twickenham. Now he has the ultimate challenge – to help England win the next World Cup. In looking back at the England tour to South Africa in 1994, he is able to look ahead to the World Cup in 1995.

What would you say was England's biggest problem in the 1993-94 season?

England took a long time to come to terms with the new laws and I think too many people spent too much time criticising them and complaining that they were unworkable and not conducive to good rugby, and too little time working out how to adapt to them and make the most of them, whatever their shortcomings.

How well did you feel England performed last season?

I thought they played with enormous spirit and huge commitment against New Zealand to deserve a famous victory, but they then had very unconvincing performances in scraping home against Scotland and in

Taking the heat out of the situation – Jack Rowell stays cool during the South African tour.

losing to Ireland. They had a very good end to the Championship with an excellent tactical win against France in Paris before playing a much more dynamic game in beating Wales. What we need to produce in the build-up to the World Cup and in the Cup itself is a blend of our three greatest attributes – the spirit we showed in the All Blacks match, the tactical appreciation of the French match and the dynamism and style of the Welsh match. If we can produce all three for 80 minutes of every match in the World Cup, then we have as good a chance as any side of reaching the final just as we did in 1991.

What are the main difficulties which confront a manager on a short tour like England's visit to South Africa?

The main problem is the same at home or away, and that is simply the difficulty of creating a cohesive team and a distinctive style. It is easier in New Zealand and Australia, because the top four or five provinces in New Zealand all play a very similar style, and so a new player can slot relatively easily into an All Black side, which makes life pretty straightforward for the coach. Similarly, in Australia it is not a major exercise to combine the talents of Queensland and New South Wales to produce 15 players all committed to the same approach and style of play. In England it is not quite so easy to blend players from several different clubs and English divisional sides into a group all geared to one distinctive style of play. Furthermore, the three major Southern Hemisphere countries benefit dramatically from their provincial system. There is no doubt that Natal or Transvaal or Queensland or Auckland would probably win the Courage First Division Championship if they were allowed to participate because their provincial rugby is of a much higher standard than British club rugby, with the possible exception of Bath. And I have to be honest and admit that I doubt Bath would find it easy to beat many of those outstanding provincial sides which comprise the Super-10 series.

But even if Bath would not be expected to beat Natal and Transvaal on successive Saturdays, surely the England Test team should have done so?

You would like to think so, but you have to remember that England had not had a single match from the middle of March until they played Natal at the end of May. In exactly that eight-week period, Natal had played eight major provincial matches and would have been good enough to take on any side in the world. I believe the standard of the top five teams in the

John Slade of
Natal won this
line-out but
Queensland took
the 1994 Super-
10 final 21-10 at
King's Park,
Durban.

ILLUSTRATION COURTESY OF I.L.N. PICTURE LIBRARY

ALWAYS ONE TO SPOT A GOOD OPENING, ONCE ARCHIE HEARD ABOUT SAVE & PROSPER UNIT TRUSTS, THERE WAS NO STOPPING HIM

If you'd like to hear more about Save & Prosper Unit Trusts, just ring us on our free Moneyline: 0800 282 101. It could be just the break you need.

SAVE & PROSPER
■ THE INVESTMENT HOUSE ■
SPONSORS OF ENGLISH RUGBY

SAVE & PROSPER GROUP LTD IS A MEMBER OF IMRO AND LAUTRO

Super-10 series would compare very favourably with the standard in this year's Five Nations Championship. Our record has to be put into perspective; our Test side only played four games together in South Africa and on successive Saturdays our opponents were Natal, Transvaal and the Springboks twice. I am quite sure there will be a few countries taking part in the 1995 World Cup who would struggle to beat Natal and Transvaal.

What was the main lesson to emerge from the tour?

My main task is to develop a style of play over the next 12 months which is peculiarly England's and obviously utilises the particular talents of our international squad to its maximum potential. That has happened ever the years since the first World Cup in New Zealand and Australia but not really in England. At the moment we are in the embryonic stage and time is not on our side, so we need to work quickly.

The other major concern is the playing conditions in South Africa. It is extremely difficult to train and play for seven days in Durban in temperatures of 80 degrees and high humidity at sea-level and the following week play in much cooler temperatures at an altitude of 6,000 feet in Johannesburg. What is more, on the firm grounds in those highly contrasting climatic conditions, Five Nations rugby as we have seen it recently does not work. We need to change our emphasis.

Part of the success of the tour was the play of Paul Hull at full-back. To succeed in South Africa, we must have a strike full-back. Originally, we chose two attacking full-backs in David Pears and Ian Hunter. When we lost them, Paul Hull took over and did very well in the role of a strike full-back. We have some tremendous attacking threequarters, some very capable running forwards, and we have the makings of a very good international side. Australia and New Zealand have produced sides with skill, pace and imagination to attack from first-phase possession. They won the first two World Cups and we will have to match them if we are to win the third World Cup. And that is my aim. I think of it sometimes in business terms, and that means that just like any director of a company, you have to have a vision of the future. My vision of the future for England is quite simple – we must compete successfully on a global scale. We must be capable of beating Australia, New Zealand and South Africa. In the last 12 months England have beaten New Zealand and South Africa so we are definitely making good progress. I am confident England will make a very bold showing at the World Cup, but whether or not we are strong enough to win it only time will tell.

WHITHER WALES?

by CLEM THOMAS

To say that Wales last season rose from the ashes like a phoenix is not far from the truth. Ever since they shared the Championship with France in 1988, which was about the time that England began to pull their socks up to become the predominant European force, Wales had been spiralling down into the gutter with a series of disastrous defeats.

So tragic was the demise of this once great and proud rugby nation that many questioned whether the problem was terminal. Wales' principal dilemma was that they possessed one of the worst administrations in world rugby. This caused Mr Vernon Pugh QC, the dynamic new chairman of the International Rugby Board and also chairman of the new caucus which took over Welsh rugby with an extraordinary coup at an extraordinary general meeting in 1993, to say that the Welsh Rugby Union, as presently constituted, was unmanageable.

Amazingly, however, all criticism of the union has disappeared, for the time being, and it is remarkable how winning the Five Nations Championship can induce such amnesia. In my opinion, Welsh rugby is still unable to manage the problems which confront it during this time of astonishing change in attitudes to competitive rugby and the amateur values.

Wales is a country which abounds in absentee landlords, in the industrial and business sense. Apart from the recently privatised Welsh

Three men responsible for the fortunes of Welsh rugby: Bob Norster (centre), Alan Davies (extreme right) and Gareth Jenkins (back to the camera).

Water and South Wales Electricity, the head offices of most major companies are in London or foreign parts, so that sponsorship is extremely hard to find at both international and club level in the Principality. This could be a severe financial inhibition, particularly in the development of club rugby, if or when the game goes professional, because I can see a time when Welsh players will be crossing the border to play for richer English clubs.

As we have seen from Llanelli's recent fiscal embarrassments, the financial future of Welsh rugby is in jeopardy. There are already fears that Cardiff, with its capital city clout, will cream off the available sponsorship and attract most of the best players. In the administrative sense, the game in Wales looks equally bleak and this will remain until the Union is reconstituted and they put in proper management structures, instead of the useless political appointments made by the second-class Welsh clubs in small parochial district elections. Time and again the small clubs return men who have little or no knowledge of what goes on beyond the narrow confines of a small group of clubs, and who can offer little professional or business experience – and, worst of all, little rugby expertise – to the job of running Welsh rugby.

The Welsh Rugby Union members should all get out their prayer mats, go down on their knees and thank their lucky stars that along came three of the wisest men that Welsh rugby has produced for some time, in the shape of the current team manager, Bob Norster, and team coaches Alan Davies and Gareth Jenkins. The Union itself had remained unconvinced of their abilities, but nine wins since the Japanese match last October and the Five Nations trophy finally forced the Union's hand and, after their return from the South Seas, the trio were appointed through to the World Cup in South Africa next June.

Many are asking the question: whither Wales now? While trying to avoid the flippancy of that famous retort by Clive Rowlands to the same question after Wales had beaten Australia in the play-off in the first World Cup – 'Going back to beat the English' – one must say that for the first time for many years there is now hope for the future.

Scott Quinnell – already a match-winner for Wales and a reason for optimism in the Welsh camp.

This opinion is shared by the team management and coaches. Alan Davies tells me that he is confident that not only are Wales going to be a hard side to beat next season, but they will be a difficult team to defeat in the 1995 World Cup. He believes that, although nothing has changed in terms of fairly limited player resources, the squad itself has developed quite remarkably. 'They know that they are the Five Nations Champions and that therefore they must be respected as such.' By ringing the changes

Richie Collins (right) of Pontypridd, now back to his best, pursues Cardiff's Mike Hall in the 1994 SWALEC Cup semi-final.

throughout the summer tour, Davies involved and developed the whole squad.

Nothing much has changed in terms of personnel, apart from the emergence last season of Scott Quinnell as a future star and the re-emergence of Richie Collins during the summer as a fiery flanker capable of some fine tackling and getting to the breakdown. Wales are now a rapidly developing side. During the summer, according to Alan Davies, the forwards simply grew and grew in stature and the backs are now confident of scoring from many situations. 'We do not attempt to use England as our benchmark, for their failure to score tries has been a major problem which could well prevent them from achieving success in the World Cup. We in Wales are looking for a different style of game which is less introverted and more expansive, and this was reflected when we were second only to France in the Five Nations over the matter of scoring tries; England managed only two tries, Wales seven and France nine.'

Davies also believes that the advantage of Southern Hemisphere physicality is a myth. 'England have matched it, so have France, and therefore so can we. I am now confident of meeting South Africa, New Zealand or Australia, particularly now that we have revamped our sporting science systems and can handle the mental and physical problems of the individual players. We can give them all private tuition whenever they need it.'

Bob Norster confirms that there is a new confidence in the Welsh team, which is now more positive and determined. 'Our biggest blemish recently was to lose to Western Samoa, when some of our players became stressed at playing in over 100 degrees and failed to contain the Samoan counter-attacks. Our forwards were equal to the task, but we went to pieces in other areas. For all that, we have pulled the squad further together. We know our strengths and weaknesses, and we know exactly what we have to work on. Above all, the players are beginning to believe in themselves and their ability to take on all the major countries.'

The future of Welsh rugby now rests on their autumn games against Italy, Romania and South Africa, and also with their Five Nations encounter with England at Cardiff. Only then will we know if they are going to be credible challengers for the World Cup.

THE SUMMER TOURS

ENGLAND STRETCHED TO THE LIMIT IN THE NEW SOUTH AFRICA

by IAN ROBERTSON, BBC Rugby Correspondent

The British Lions discovered last year on their tour to New Zealand that there is no such thing as an easy match. They lost six of their 13 matches and learned the painful lesson that on the new formula of short tours they play only the best provincial sides, which stretches them to the limits not just on Saturdays, but in the midweek games as well. This state of affairs was confirmed on England's eight-match tour to South Africa with only three victories to set against five defeats.

The enormity of the task facing England was known the moment the tour itinerary was announced. They had two Saturday games against the top two provinces in South Africa, Natal and Transvaal, with two Test matches on the other two Saturdays, while the midweek games, featuring primarily the England reserve team, included games against Orange Free State and the South Africa A selection.

A hard task was made even harder by the sharp contrast in preparation made by the England team and their opponents. The England midweek team had never played together before arriving in Durban and the Test side had not played as a unit since the middle of March – a break of eight weeks. More to the point, in that eight-week period, Natal and Transvaal had each played eight major matches, at least half of them in the extremely high-powered and competitive Super-10 series. This is a relatively new competition which takes place over six weeks from the end of March until the middle of May, featuring one South Pacific side (Western Samoa), two from Australia (Queensland and New South Wales), three from South Africa (Natal, Transvaal and Eastern Province) and four from New Zealand (Auckland, Otago, North Harbour and Waikato). The standard of these outstanding sides is incredibly high and after playing each other over a six-week period they were at their very best to face an international side like England on their tour of South Africa or Ireland on their tour of Australia.

I firmly believe that the best of these provincial teams – Queensland, Natal, Transvaal or Auckland – would have been good enough to have won the 1994 Five Nations Championship. That is not a criticism of the

Time off for the tourists and an opportunity for a team safari (left) and a solo performance by Brian Moore at Sun City (below).

Facing page:
Rob Andrew's
opportunist try in
the First Test in
Pretoria.

Five Nations but a genuine appreciation of the fantastic standard of the Super-10 series.

This puts into perspective the challenge which faced England as they prepared at sea-level in Durban in temperatures of over 80 degrees for their opening match at an appropriate altitude against Orange Free State in Bloemfontein. It is accepted in South Africa that there are two ways to adjust to playing at high altitude. The first is to spend at least a fortnight training at high altitude before playing there. The alternative is to fly in the the day before. England chose the second option, but they were unlucky in that not only were they hit by the altitude but the temperature in Bloemfontein touched the mid-70s, which is very unusual in May. They were also hit by an aggressive, fired-up Free State, who played some pretty good rugby to beat England 22-11.

Even in defeat, Paul Hull had a wonderful match at full-back, making one particularly glorious break which led to a try scored by Hopley. Although it was disappointing to lose, England took some comfort from the fact that they had fielded the entire reserve XV and better things might be expected from the Test team against Natal. In fact, things got much worse. England lost 21-6 in a match of nine penalties. The forwards were outplayed and made to look rather slow on the fast, dry pitch and the hot and humid conditions had a debilitating effect.

On the Sunday, England were literally and metaphorically licking their wounds. Two defeats in two matches, and the first-choice full-back, David Pears, was ruled out of the remainder of the tour with a sprung rib cartilage. There were also injuries to Rob Andrew (five stitches in a head wound), Dean Richards (muscle spasms in his back) and Mike Catt (shoulder strain).

Will Carling is
tackled by Japie
Mulder as
England go down
to Transvaal at
Ellis Park.

At this point the management felt it was essential to win the third game, against Western Transvaal in Potchefstroom. They picked what turned out to be six of their Test side to bolster the usual midweek dirt-trackers side. They included Paul Hull, Will Carling and Tony Underwood in the backs and Martin Bayfield, Nigel Redman and Ben Clarke in the forwards. This bold selection was rewarded with a narrow but well-deserved win by 26 points to 24.

The Transvaal game always threatened to be impossibly difficult, and so it proved. Although both sides scored two tries, the referee was much more generous in awarding penalties to Transvaal and they took full advantage to win 24-21. In fairness to them, they did play some excellent running rugby and they were especially dangerous on the counter-attack.

Another defeat was to follow in midweek when the reserve side lost to South Africa A in Kimberley by 19-16. This match was a guide to the comparative strengths of the two national reserve squads but it had virtually no bearing on the outcome of the Test. After they lost to two well-organised provincial sides on the two previous Saturdays, it was fascinating to learn that the England players genuinely believed it would be much easier for them to beat the scratch South African side in the Test. The Springboks would inevitably lack the cohesion and collective skills of Natal and Transvaal, even though they might be better individually, and there was no doubt that England went into the Test full of optimism.

The Pretoria Test will forever be known as Rob Andrew's Test. He set a new English record by scoring 27 points in a truly magnificent victory. His points came from one try, one dropped goal, two conversions and five penalties. The other try for England was scored by Ben Clarke. Andrew played one of his very best internationals, dominating the stage at Loftus Versfeld in Pretoria and controlling the game tactically. His goal-kicking was quite exceptional, he set a new world record with his 19th dropped goal at international level and he scored a splendid try when he followed up a high kick and plucked the ball out of the air under the nose of the Springbok full-back to score only his second try for England. His tackling and his tactical kicking were both as stunning as ever but he would be the first to agree that the real heroes were the forwards. They were in devastating form and they totally overwhelmed the South African pack. They outscrummaged them, had much the better of the line-out and were far quicker, more incisive and more creative in the open.

The season had begun so well with a marvellous victory over New Zealand at Twickenham in November and now they had destroyed South Africa in Pretoria. They confirmed that when they hit top form they are as good as any side in the world. Yet this superb win by England was only part of

Ben Clarke goes over for England's first try at the beginning of a devastating 20 minutes.

An historic occasion as Will Carling meets President Nelson Mandela before the Test match in Pretoria.

the story of a memorable and historic day. This was the first major international sporting event to take place in South Africa since the first-ever democratic elections, held just a few weeks previously. Before the kick-off both teams were introduced to the new President, Nelson Mandela, and the Deputy State President, F.W. de Klerk. Such was the charisma and mystique of Mr Mandela that the whole England touring party joined the 21 players and replacements on the pitch to meet the State President. It was a highly charged emotional occasion which no one who was there will ever forget. The match was an expression of the national unity of the new South Africa and there was a wonderful ovation given to both F.W. de Klerk and Nelson Mandela – but especially to Nelson Mandela, surely one of the greatest and most influential politicians of the 20th century.

Sadly, the theme of peace and friendship conceived on the Saturday was still-born on the Tuesday in Port Elizabeth. In a very nasty, ill-tempered match which was ruined by some very weak refereeing, the Eastern Province players were guilty of some desperate provocation. Jon Callard received 25 stitches in two gaping head wounds after one of the locks, van der Berg, stood on him. Van der Berg was very fortunate not to be sent off, and so too was the hooker, Jaco Kirsten. England's Tim Rodber and Eastern Province's Simon Tremain were not so fortunate. Tremain launched an appalling attack on Rodber, who retaliated. Both were sent off. Rodber was far more sinned against than sinning and there were a dozen far worse incidents in the match which the referee chose to ignore, but nonetheless Tremain and Rodber could not complain about their treatment.

Eastern Province were a poor side who resorted to playing dirty rugby and I'm delighted to say that they got their deserts. England won 31-13. Paul Hull, the real discovery of the tour, scored two tries and Steve Bates got the other.

Unfortunately, that was to be England's last win of the tour. In 1993 the British Lions had enjoyed a crushing win over the All Blacks in Wellington in the Second Test to go into the Third Test the following week as hot favourites. They found they could not scale the heights, could not peak two weeks in a row. Similarly, England climbed Everest in Pretoria but they could not repeat their heroics the following week in Cape Town. The revamped South African pack, which showed five changes from the First Test, outplayed England. At the end of a very long and demanding season the English players looked tired, played out and in need of a rest. They made the supreme effort in Pretoria; they couldn't repeat it in Cape Town. They lost by 27-9.

A victory over the Springboks on their own soil is an achievement to be celebrated in style.

But there is no denying that the whole trip was worthwhile. The experience of playing and training for a month in different parts of South Africa will be invaluable for the World Cup. They now know the problems of excessive heat and high humidity and also the difficulties of playing at high altitude. Manager Jack Rowell also knows the likely make-up of his World Cup squad. He was delighted that a large group of the reserve squad made a real impact and proved they are ready for promotion to bigger and better challenges. Of the backs, Paul Hull had an outstanding tour and he is unquestionably a player with a great future ahead of him. Mike Catt was given more exposure at this higher level and he acquitted himself really well. Of the forwards, Steve Ojomoh had an excellent tour and both reserve props, Graham Rowntree and Nick Mallett, showed they were ready for international rugby.

At the start of last season the England captain, Will Carling, would probably have been pretty pleased if he had been told that England would beat New Zealand in November, South Africa in June and would win three of the four Five Nations games in between. This season they will expect to beat Romania and Canada before Christmas, win the Five Nations after Christmas and, at the very worst, reach the last four in the World Cup. And who knows, if they reproduce the form they showed in Pretoria they could well reach the World Cup final in 1995 just as they did in 1991.

THE OTHER TOURS

by BILL MITCHELL

The Northern Hemisphere had mixed results from tours undertaken during the close season – if there is such a thing nowadays. France, Wales and Italy enjoyed the best results while Ireland and Scotland, the latter seriously weakened by unavailable players, possibly wished they had never undertaken their visits to Australia and Argentina respectively.

FRANCE IN CANADA AND NEW ZEALAND

France took themselves off to Canada and New Zealand and started off by experiencing a shock in North America as they not only struggled to beat the USA Eagles but then lost the full international against Canada, thanks to the boot of Gareth Rees, who scored all the home team's points in their 18-16 win in Ottawa. To add insult to injury the French augmented their 'bad boys' with their ninth dismissal – none other than Philippe Sella in his 99th match for his country. Canada also had a player ordered to the showers: hooker Mark Cardinal in the first half. Sella 'walked' for alleged punching with some 11 minutes to go, while Cardinal's offence was stamping; both players received derisory sentences and who is surprised by that? These are the days when heavy penalties for foul play are studiously avoided.

French captain Philippe Saint-André (below) is tackled by All Black Matt Cooper in the Second Test at Eden Park.

The French did, however, shrug off that indignity and the New Zealand section of the tour brought only two more defeats and, more significantly, a 2-0 Test series success over the All Blacks starting with a marvellous 22-8 win in the First Test in Christchurch. The series was clinched in Auckland a week later thanks to a late try by full-back Sadourny in a narrow 23-20 victory.

Sadourny was one of several French players who made themselves front runners for the

1995 World Cup squad, others being wing Emile N'Tamack, Thierry Lacroix, skipper Philippe Saint-André, fly-half Christophe Deylaud, new scrum-half Guy Accocebery and the established forwards Benetton, Benazzi and Cabannes. Philippe Sella played his 100th and 101st games for France, a record which will take some beating, particularly as he is not yet too close to retirement.

WELSH SUMMER CAMPAIGN

Wales played no fewer than seven games during the 'break' and won six of them including 102-11 and 54-0 World Cup qualifying wins in Portugal and Spain respectively. Then the team had two more successes in Canada, including a 33-15 win over the home country to avenge their shock 26-24 defeat in November in Cardiff. They then set off for the South Seas and took on Fiji, Tonga and Western Samoa in full Tests over eight days. The first two matches brought 23-8 and 18-9 wins, but the latter was a dull affair which suggested that fatigue was setting in and Western Samoa proved the point by winning the Apia Test 34-9. But it was a more than useful exercise for Wales as they were able to blood new players, including scrum-half John, hooker McBryde, wing Wilkins, number 8 Steve Williams and prop Ian Buckett, who were given the chance to play in the cauldron – almost literally – of international rugby. It can also only have improved team spirit, not always a strong point with Welsh sides in recent seasons.

A 2-0 series win and the French celebrations begin, led by Olivier Roumat and Abdel Benazzi.

Nigel Davies (with the ball) and Neil Jenkins helped Wales to overwhelm Spain in their World Cup qualifier in Madrid, to the delight of their travelling supporters.

ITALY IN AUSTRALIA

Italy undertook a tough tour of Australia and should take considerable satisfaction from their efforts out there. Of their seven games only the two Tests were lost – the First in Brisbane by a narrow 23-20 scoreline and the Second by 20-7 in Melbourne. Australia had their strongest available teams on show and the Italians looked like plausible challengers for the future. Watch out in the World Cup for the South African-bred Cuttitta brothers, full-back Vaccari and fly-half Troiani among others. They must – like the French – continue to try disciplinary improvements as too often they were involved in brawls and foul play.

IRELAND IN AUSTRALIA

Ireland won only two of their eight matches in Australia and both were hollow successes. The two Tests – in Brisbane and Sydney – were lost by 33-13 and 32-18 respectively and the other defeats were catastrophic, the 29-26 loss in Brisbane against Queensland being the only exception. The only reasonable successes amongst the players were newcomers Bell from Loughborough University in the centre, wing Nial Woods, hooker Wood and flanker Corkery from Cork Constitution. Others did little to enhance their reputations, but the Irish do have a nasty habit of bouncing back from disaster so Five Nations opponents at least should read nothing into their tour results.

SCOTLAND IN ARGENTINA

In Argentina Scotland did no better than the Irish in Australia with half their recognised international side absent. Only one match in six was won – at Cordoba – with one drawn and the series was lost by small margins in each Test in Buenos Aires, 16-15 and 19-17.

In fact, better place-kicking would have brought success instead of failure on each occasion and in the First Test in particular Gregor Townsend was culpable in taking the wrong options from stand-off, which might have made a big difference.

Certain players were given a run in the international arena and would seem to be fine future prospects, notably the Melrose wing Craig Joiner, their scrum-half Bryan Redpath, the Gala full-back Michael Dods (although his kicking could have been better) and the barely established prop Alan Sharp, flanker Peter Walton and number 8 Carl Hogg. The

Hogg (8), McKenzie (2) and Sharp (far right) stand by as Argentinians Llanes (4) and Noriega (3) take control and Scotland lose the Second Test .

experience in unfamiliar surroundings for them and others can only bring its own benefits.

BARBARIANS IN ZIMBABWE

The Barbarians also flew the flag by playing three matches in Zimbabwe, losing only to the national team, by 23-21 in Harare, but as we go to press many clubs will be warming up for the season by making ambitious trips and we hope they did well. They need the experience and the hosts, particularly in the less rugby-orientated places, need their visits to promote the game.

All Black captain Sean Fitzpatrick watches as his South African counterpart, François Pienaar, signs a ball for New Zealand Prime Minister John Bolger.

SOUTH AFRICA IN NEW ZEALAND

South Africa won ten of their 14 matches in New Zealand and lost three with one draw, which meant that they were not whitewashed in the series, won 2-0 by the All Blacks. Better discipline might have meant victories in all three Tests. Against Waikato the wing, James Small, was guilty of a dreadful tackle; against Manawatu lock Adri Geldenhuys was sent off and in the Second Test the prop Johan le Roux was found on television evidence to have bitten All Black skipper Sean Fitzpatrick.

When they did move the ball they looked very good, especially in the Third Test in Auckland, but their general niggly behaviour made them no friends and they have much to do before the World Cup if they are to win it.

WESTERN SAMOA IN AUSTRALIA

Western Samoa, on a five-match tour to Australia, won their first four games and then suffered a fearsome 73-3 thrashing at the hands of the Wallabies in Sydney. One hopes that this catastrophe, in which 11 tries were conceded, will not do them untold harm in the World Cup.

LOOKING BACK

25 YEARS AGO
from the pages of *Rugby World*

compiled by NIGEL STARMER-SMITH

January 1970

My own experience among the schools this season has been confined to the south of England, but in that area there appear to be many centres of ability and promise well above the average. They include S.R.T. Penniston of Rugby, perhaps the most promising of all, D.O. Casswell (Christ's Hospital), G.E. Wood (Uppingham), M. Wilson-Smith (Wellington College), T.A. Hewlett (Oundle), J.R. Wells (Epsom), S.E. West (Cranbrook) and E.J.D. Clarke, who should have one and perhaps two more years at Harrow. To these might be added the name of P.J. Warfield, the Haileybury captain. Among other players who have impressed me are full-backs P.J.E. Needham (Harrow) and G. Hinton (Tiffin); wing threequarters N.E. McCorquodale (Harrow), D. Moss-Bowpitt (Tiffin) and L.E. Urena (Eastbourne); fly-half N. Bennett (Tiffin); scrum-halves R.P.C. Dickson (Eastbourne) and B.M. Smith (Epsom); and forwards P.H. Edmonds (Cranbrook), G.M. Cryer and R.F. Looker (Dulwich), S.A. Johnson (Christ's Hospital), R.C. Symonett (The Leys), C.W. Owen and J.P. Dickins (Oundle) and S.J. Ashcroft (Uppingham).
Geoff Abbott

England have taken at least two revolutionary steps. They have appointed an official coach to the national team, Don White, and for the match against the Springboks at Twickenham they nominated Bob Hiller (Harlequins) as captain several weeks in advance. In addition, they arranged a number of weekend coaching sessions for the national squad. All this at least argues progressive thinking, and if it produced results, in the shape of an improved performance by the England team, Mr Albert Agar and his co-selectors will deserve every congratulation.
Vivian Jenkins

Bob Hiller, appointed captain of England for the match against the Springboks.

Noel Henderson, though near the veteran stage, scored the match-winning try for Ireland against Australia in the last minute of their match in 1958.

As he wearily left the field to the plaudits of the crowd, a press photographer came up to him and said:

'Noel, you're losing your speed.'

'But I got there, didn't I,' replied Noel.

'Sure,' said the photographer, 'but when David Hewitt gave you the ball at halfway, I took your picture taking the pass, and damn me if I wasn't behind the try-line to take you again as you put the ball down. And I was carrying a camera!'

Come to Colombes with *Rugby World*

• • • • • • • • • • •

Here is your chance to see what may well be the most exciting international match of the season - France v England in Paris on April 18 - and because of the special arrangements, Rugby World has made with Beaupol Travel Ltd., you can be assured of a worry-free trip. A high standard of hotel has been chosen and, apart from pocket money, the only extras will be lunch on the Saturday and Sunday. Everything else is included.

* Depart Friday, April 17; return Sunday, April 19.
* Direct flight from Gatwick to Paris.
* 2 nights accommodation in the 3-star (A) Hotel Garnier in the centre of the city.
* Transfers to and from Colombes Stadium.
* Breakfasts, dinners and match ticket all included.
* ALL FOR £27 PER PERSON

Llanelli's proud boast is that their Youth team is the best in the land. Their record after 11 matches was certainly remarkable: 430 points for and 47 against, and all 11 matches won. One unfortunate side was walloped 115-3, Llanelli scoring 20 goals and five tries.

The team was formed six years ago and has since had a steady flow of talent into the senior side. Current members include the brothers Clive and Alan John, Derek Quinnell and Helin Jenkins.

Now the Youth, expertly coached by the former Llanelli fly-half, Peter Lewis, are eagerly looking forward to their match with Llandovery College, which will be staged as a curtain-raiser to the Llanelli-South Africans match at Stradey in January.

February 1970

Charlie Hannaford, the Cambridge Blue, who at present teaches at Sherborne and plays for Rosslyn Park, is taking up a new post at Clifton College next September.

Bristol would obviously be his nearest club, but Hannaford, a brilliant No. 8 who has several times played for Gloucestershire, has not yet decided whether to play for them or his native Gloucester.

Brian Stevens, the Penzance and Newlyn prop who played for England against South Africa at Twickenham, is the first Cornish forward to win international honours since the great Vic Roberts in 1951.

A farmer in the south-western corner of the county, 'Stack' Stevens is a tough, mobile player who had a big hand in Cornwall's journey to the county championship final last season.

Welsh international John O'Shea has been made manager of Courage (Western) Ltd, depot and will be living in Penzance.

The Cardiff captain and Lions forward, who will be taking up his appointment in mid-March, is no stranger to West Country Rugby. A one-time student at St Luke's College, Exeter, O'Shea has toured with Welsh Academicals and Captain Crawshay's XV.

The Pirates, naturally, are hoping that he will be turning out at the Mennaye Field, but at least two other Cornish clubs have hopes that O'Shea will be joining them.

His rugged features, dark curly hair and flashing eyes make him look like a high-ranking bandit from Sicily. But, in fact, he is a quiet citizen, devoted to rugby football. His main aim as a flank forward is to seek the ball and win it for his backs and, failing that, to get near the opposing line and score tries.

David Morris, of Neath, is a tremendous trier. Several years before he won his first cap, in 1967, he was spotted as a player of

Dai Morris with the ball for Wales against Scotland at Cardiff in 1968.

must be put in so that 'it first touches the ground immediately beyond the width of the nearer prop's shoulders'.

This means, in effect, that no loose-head hooker can raise his foot to strike for the ball until it has bounced virtually below his left shoulder.

I defy any hooker to get the ball legally in such circumstances. If he waits until the ball has bounced before he lifts his foot to strike, he will be too late, and the ball will have gone past him.
Vivian Jenkins

promise. Yet he was always the silent, smiling one who stood at the back of the group and never pushed himself into the limelight.

Pressmen recognised his ability on the field, but could never get beneath his protecting veil of modesty. Among his team colleagues he was liked and respected, and success on the field playing for Wales has not changed his approach or attitude.

In his opinion, Welsh rugby is the best in the world. He says: 'I do not think that any club outside the Principality can maintain the high standard of play and survive against the physical combat required to win the Welsh unofficial championship.'
J B G Thomas

March 1970

Stuffy, pig-headed, pompous... These are some of the epithets one hears applied from time to time to the members of the International Board, and no doubt they resent them. But there really are times when they lead with their chins.

Some years ago, for instance, they brought in an amendment to the hooking law which everyone – except the Board – agrees is unworkable. It lays down that no front-row players 'may raise or advance a foot until the ball has touched the ground', together with the restriction that the ball

The emergence of Loughborough University, once the technological part of an overall Colleges set-up at Loughborough, created the other interest. Like Surrey, Loughborough started with at least one well-known player when they first became a full university, in 1965 – the English trialist and UAU hooker, J.J. Elliott, now with Leicester.

The Welsh games, keen as ever, saw the two Northern colleges, Aberystwyth and Bangor, head the list, with UWIST in Cardiff perhaps unlucky to come third.

A big exodus of top Rugby Union players to League has left Australia facing a difficult task in building up for the coming season's matches with Scotland and with those against South Africa in 1971.

Australia's stock has never been so low at international level, and the unprecedented turnover of players is reflected in the fact that the Wallabies have won only one of their last 14 Tests.

Seven of the 1966-67 Wallabies to tour the British Isles, including five backs, had switched to Rugby League before the end of 1969. Another 15 were unavailable for selection for South Africa last year because of retirement, injury or studies.

Since the South African tour, big money offers have tempted Wallabies John Ballesty, Phil Smith and Peter Reilly to switch to League. Other potential caps who

have turned professional include centre Owen O'Donnell, scrum-half Peter Brown and big forwards Alan Kennington and Dennis Becby.
Eddie Kann

In Buenos Aires, visited by Scotland last year and Wales the year before, there are about 45 rugby clubs - which means some 8,700 players.

Rosario has 18 clubs (2,800 players) and another important province, Cordoba, has 17 clubs.

Technically, Mike Davis can now claim to have been an England captain - admittedly for only four minutes, when Bob Hiller went off the field with an injury against South Africa at Twickenham.

Davis, a well-known figure in West Country rugby – he played for Torquay and Devonport Services – currently scales 17 stone. His wife recently presented him with a baby.

Incidentally, Tony Bucknall, back-row forward and new England cap in that memorable victory over the Springboks, was born at Torquay.

April 1970
It is with some dismay that one learns of the proposed new rota system for pairings in international fixtures. One can anticipate that, in computing fixtures this way, television coverage will be given to no more than three matches in a season.

Rugby is a participator sport, and is it not fair to believe that television is catering for the needs of a vast majority who would not brave the elements anyway? Times have changed and, in these days of sophisticated habits, followers of the game will not be lured back to the terraces.

If it is falling attendances to which the clubs point, then surely this is no criticism of television but a sign of the times in which we live.
M Wilkins,
Lydney, Glos.

Left: Bonzo Johns of Redruth.
Far left: Mike Davies (left) with his younger brother Brian.

That great West Country character, 'Bonzo' Johns, is threatening to retire from County Championship rugby. I understand he is making himself available for the return match against France B, in Cornwall at that end of the season, and then proposes to call it a day as a county player.

He will, however, continue to turn out for his club, Redruth. When he ran out against Camborne recently, Bonzo was making his 650th appearance for the Reds.

A mere three hookers have played for Scotland in the country's last 59 internationals, and of these three – Norman Bruce, Derek Deans and Frank Laidlaw – Deans has as yet only the one cap he gained

Tony O'Reilly on tour in New Zealand.

against England at Murrayfield in 1968, when Laidlaw withdrew with ligament trouble in a knee.

At 29 years of age, Frank Laidlaw, with 27 caps, has nicely in his sights the record number for a Scotland hooker – namely, 31 standing to the name of Norman Bruce – especially as, beyond this season's Calcutta Cup there is an additional cap on offer against Australia in the course of Scotland's short summer tour.

Even the full Scottish record, the 40 caps apiece of Hughie McLeod and David Rollo, is rapidly coming into range, for, as Sam Hodgson of England and the Lions was wont to prove, his 30s need be no barrier to a class hooker.
Norman Mair

Tony O'Reilly's dramatic return to representative rugby, when he played for Ireland as a last-minute replacement against England at Twickenham, was one of the most talked-about events of the season – and small wonder.

It is not every day that a £20,000-a-year executive, with six children, comes back at the age of 33 to international rugby. His last appearance against England at Twickenham had been in 1960.

Yet he must have wondered, after his reappearance, whether it had been worth while. He never received a pass throughout the afternoon, and spent most of his time throwing the ball in from touch.

On the few occasions when he was given the chance of chasing a diagonal kick-ahead, he looked heavier and slower into his stride than he had in his prime; and a bump on the head which laid him out for two or three minutes late in the second half can hardly have helped.

Fortunately, he still retains his sense of humour, which is legendary. 'When I came to,' he said, 'the first thing I saw was the scoreboard; but I thought it read: "Ireland 9, England 3", instead of the other way round. I wish I'd gone back to sleep again!'

England, of course, won by 9 points to 3, thanks chiefly to those two wonderful dropped goals by Bob Hiller.
Vivian Jenkins

The announcement that All Black prop Ken Gray has retired from the first-class game and will devote his future to family and farming has come as an unpleasant surprise.

Gray, who at the age of 29 has retired seemingly at the height of his powers, was – with due respect to Wilson Whineray – the best scrummaging prop in the All Black teams of the last decade.
Donald Cameron

May 1970

Nigel Starmer-Smith's original club, Gosford All Blacks of Kidlington, Oxford, made history recently when it became the first rugby club in Great Britain to entertain and play a team from HM Prison Springhill, near Aylesbury, Bucks.

The prisoners arrived in an official coach; their team included three warders, and it was a good, hard match – 'the cleanest I have played in the season,' according to one Gosford player.

Congratulations to Delme Thomas, who seems to have been so successful in overcoming the gravitational problems so that beset the normal line-out jumper that he can remain suspended in mid-air for seconds on end.

When will international referees wake up to the fact that Thomas's feats of levitation have less to do with mind over matter than with unfair coaching tactics?
N. K. J. Witney,
Corpus Christi College, Oxford

Welshman Gwynne Walters is convinced that neutral referees for all international matches, and not just those involving the home countries, will come in the 1970s. 'It's the only way', he says, 'to avoid the unpleasantness which touring sides from the British Isles have experienced abroad.'

Walters' opinion is worth noting, for during a distinguished refereeing career he handled 22 international and seven 'Varsity' matches.

Now he is in retirement and confesses to a growing worry over the variety of interpretations of some of rugby's complex laws. 'This is something we must endeavour to put right,' he says. 'As things stand at the moment, even the law-makers are not always 100 per cent sure of their ground.'

June 1970
Geoff Cooke is to take over from his co-centre, Philip Carter, as Bradford's captain next season.

Cooke, who has captained the Cumberland Westmoreland side, is one of three county skippers in Bradford's current team. The others are Carter and scrum-half Roger Pickering, who have both led Yorkshire.

July 1970
I read with deep shock of the International Board's decision to ban J.A.T. Rodd, the Scottish international, from playing rugby in Board countries. The idea of the Board agreeing this absurd decision was, to me, incredible, and if it is a democratic body, the future of the game at the top seems bleak indeed.

I suppose A.F.J. O'Reilly should now be prevented playing because he wrote an article in the England v Ireland programme, and surely Andy Mulligan must be barred, as he is also a journalist and still playing for London Irish in a junior side last season.
Julian K B Deale,
Blackrock, Dublin

Four well-known players who all started their careers with the Chelmsford club are England internationals Tony Bucknall (Richmond) and Mike Bulpitt (Blackheath), Jeremy Janion (Bedford), a final England trialist along with Bucknall and Bulpitt, and Dave Mackay, now with Rosslyn Park.

All four appeared last season in the successful Eastern Counties side – and Chelmsford doubt if any other club of their standing can boast such a record.

Next season this progressive Essex club celebrates its 50th anniversary. President Hanbury Allen has been a member since its formation in 1920.

August 1970
Last season was the first in which the Ireland XV trained and planned under the direction of an officially recognised coach – Ronnie Dawson – and it was also the first season in which the four Provinces, Ulster, Munster, Leinster and Connacht, appointed coaches and picked squads for additional training sessions.

As it happened, Leinster confirmed Dawson as their coach some months before the Irish Rugby Football Union finally named him to take charge of the international side. In future, I understand, the intention is that the duties of the national coach will not overlap with those of any of the provincial coaches.

Individual flair has always meant a great deal in Irish rugby, and the present side owes much to the instinctive greatness of players like Tom Kiernan, Alan Duggan, Michael Gibson, Ken Goodall and Bill McBride. The success of future teams will depend largely on the appearance of a new crop of equally gifted performers, players who must be given every opportunity to express themselves.
Peter McMullan

Scotland's six-match tour of Australia, which opened so promisingly in Melbourne with a 34-0 victory over Victoria (reported in last month's *Rugby World*), ended in a big disappointment for the visitors but helped restore rugby prestige and boost morale down under.

Scotland won only three games, scored 109 points to 94, and went down 3-23 against Australia before a crowd of 26,930 at the Sydney Cricket Ground.

This was the second-biggest defeat Australia had inflicted on a team in an international match. The biggest was in 1931, when the Wallabies had a 31-6 victory in their second international match against the Maoris, at Palmerston North in New Zealand.

After their long flight from London, and with insufficient time to adjust themselves to the weather and playing conditions, the Scots showed in flashes only that they were better than their Australian record suggested.

They were hampered, too, by injuries to full-back Ian Smith and to their hookers, skipper Frank Laidlaw and Derek Deans, while a depressed cheekbone fracture in the opening match put Tom Elliot out for the rest of the tour. Laidlaw, injured a week before the international match, recovered just in time to lead Scotland.
Eddie Kann

September 1970

Until he retired recently from his work in London and went to live at Barry, Ronnie Boon was the astute honorary secretary of London Welsh. He has not, however, cut himself adrift from English rugby. Indeed, he is working with all his old zeal as chairman of the 37 leading clubs who wish to start a top-class competition.

With Boon's drive behind the movement, I have no doubt we shall see competitive rugby among the top clubs very soon, even though it is not yet an accomplished fact after more than a year of discussion.

The Rugby Union rejected the 37 clubs' application for recognition of their competition, and itself outlined a competitive scheme to representatives of 66 clubs – including, of course, most of the 37 – whom they invited to a conference early in July.
J B G Thomas

Bob Hiller, of Harlequins, who has scored over 1,700 points in seven seasons of first-class rugby, has been acclaimed as one of the greatest place-kickers of all time; but Hiller will have to score that many points again in the years remaining to him in the first-class game if he is to equal – let alone surpass – the points tally of Coventry's George Cole.

Cole, in a first-class career which has spanned 16 seasons and taken in nearly 500 games for Coventry, Warwickshire and the Barbarians, has reaped a harvest of close on 3,500 points, most of them from kicks. It is a record of matchless consistency and one which, surely, marks him out as the most prolific points-scorer in the history of the game.
David Kenny

It was in England, after all, that the game originated, and it is the Rugby Union's centenary, not anyone else's, that is being celebrated. But no doubt the hope is that many of the principles that dominate the RU's thinking will rub off on the delegates from the 'new' Rugby countries of the world.

The first of these principles, no doubt – especially with Mr Bill Ramsay, the president of the Rugby Union, in the chair – is that the game should remain essentially and irreversibly amateur. In other words, it should be regarded as a spare-time occupation, a relief from the player's ordinary work, and a recreation, in the truest sense of the word, instead of becoming an over-obsessive activity that interferes with job and home.

Within these bounds it is still possible for a man to play extremely good rugby, and even if he is only a moderate performer, or an out-and-out 'rabbit' he can still get immense fun and companionship from the game.

It is the 'third half', in the clubhouse afterwards, that lifts rugby above many other games in the world. Thus lifelong friendships are forged.

It is all very well to talk of 'World Cups' and such-like, but for an amateur, whose time is strictly limited, these things are not feasible.

Only a professional, whose job is involved, can afford the time, and the money, to take part in such things.
Vivian Jenkins

A visitor to Lingfield Park racecourse recently would have seen some unusual jumping over the hurdles, inasmuch as the jumpers were members of the Richmond club – attired in morning dress and toppers!

The occasion was the reception, held on the racecourse, following the wedding at Forest Row of Brian Stoneman (England trialist, Barbarian, Oxford and Richmond forward) to Miss Joy Bowen.

Seven of the bridegroom's Richmond friends decided to stage a race of two-and-a-half furlongs over the hurdles. The 'runners' were Bill Munks, former

Richmond president and captain; Ernie Preece, former club captain; John Power-Rees, ex-captain of the Vikings XV; John Aarvold, first XV forward; Bob Vallings, the A XV captain, and Rob Robins, prop forward.

Another would-be 'runner', John Taylor, Vikings' full-back, was disqualified as he was 'not properly attired for the race', not being in morning dress.

The event was won by Vallings, with Preece second.

Efforts by players to change clubs caused the French Rugby Federation's president, M Albert Ferrasse, to refer to 'a wind of folly' at the Federation's annual congress, held at Perpignan during the close season.

The problem worried him, he said. All club directors must understand the harm these moves did to the game. If he has proof of any of them recruiting for players, he would act 'with great severity'.

This was generally interpreted as 'I would have them suspended for life'. Knowing this, the recruiters take care they are not found out. The approaches are made by associates who have nothing at stake.

M Ferrasse quoted a letter he had received from an official of the Irish Rugby Union emphasising the 'absolute necessity to maintain amateurism'.

If discipline was not imposed, there would be an end to the rugby at which the Federation aimed.

About brutal rugby, M Ferrasse said there was a slight drop last season, but there was still far too much of it. On the scorning of referees, he has heard these officials spoken of as 'the sun and the rain'. They should be accepted just as the sun and rain are accepted during play.

Douglas William Cumming Smith went to Australia and New Zealand in 1950 as a member of one of the finest set of backs the British Lions have ever sent abroad, a set that included these illustrious names – Jackie Kyle, Bleddyn Williams, Jack Matthews and Ken Jones.

Next year Duggie Smith returns to New Zealand as manager of the Lions, and he believes that the men behind the scrum he will be able to take can be rated even better than those who went 20 years ago.

It has always been impossible to compare one era with another, but one can

RFU president Bill Ramsey with Chancellor of the Exchequer Iain McLeod at the 1963 Calcutta Cup match at Twickenham.

see reason in Duggie's confidence. 'I believe we have the best chance Britain has ever had of winning a Test series in New Zealand', he said to me. These are the words of a canny Scot, remember, one not given to overplaying his hand or talking big for the sake of it.

'We will have much better backs than New Zealand,' says Smith, 'and I have to find forwards who can win the ball for them. I want big, strong front-row men who are mobile. Every forward must be fast and able to run with the ball. The back-row will be easy enough to find but the front and middle rows must be able to run, too, and the middle row must jump. That's

where my problem is. Where are the jumpers who are runners as well?

'I know I am asking for the moon, but if I get half of it I am sure we can be the first Lions to win a Test series. The whole party must have the will to win.'
Rupert Cherry

The oldest hoodoo in the long history of Springboks-All Blacks Rugby remains unbroken. The touring side has never yet won the opening international match of a series and, in defiance of almost every forecast, South Africa pulled it off at Pretoria on July 25 with a show of comprehensive authority.

It may have made surprising reading, too, in the British Isles. The manner in which the Springboks took their grip on this match, to win by 17-6, surely made those ghastly upsets of the recent British Isles tour seem unbelievably remote.

For New Zealand, it meant the end of an historic run of success: 15 successive international victories and an overall tally of 55 matches without defeat.

At the Rugby Football Union's annual meeting on July 10, held at the London Hilton Hotel, W.C. (Bill) Ramsay was elected president for the 1970-71 centenary year. Dr T.A. Kemp and R.M.A. Kingswell were re-elected vice-presidents.

The Union's surplus for the 1969-70 season, after taxation was £14,279.

Ken Goodall of Ireland, Stuart Gallacher of Wales, and Bryan West of England, three of the outstanding forwards of last season's international matches, have gone over to the Rugby League, and some people seem to regard it as a disaster. 'How can we now hope to beat the All Blacks next year?', they ask.

I prefer to look at it as did Rob Oakes, that great former stalwart of the Union game in Yorkshire. A one-time England forward, he was hon. secretary of the county for 45 years, from 1907-08 until 1952-53, and knew more about the Rugby League than any other Union administrator I have known. He had to operate right in the middle of it – yet it never worried him if some leading Union player suddenly decided to change codes.

'It's the best safety valve we have', he used to say. 'Those who want to play for money can play for money, and good luck to them. But we, in the Union game, want to play for fun, as a relaxation from our jobs. *Vivian Jenkins*

October 1970

The Rugby Football Schools' Union was formed on September 1 through the amalgamation of the English Schools' RFU and the schools section of the RFU. Each of the counties affiliated to the new union will have three elected members, representing the 19 Group, the 15 Group and the independent schools.

From a playing angle, the new Union will be inaugurated on October 10 at Twickenham, where two matches will be played. Great efforts will be made to ensure that this is a successful event in the Rugby Union's centenary year, and it is hoped that the schools, in particular, will give full support.

The first game will be the 71st of the series, which started in 1904, between the English Schools (15 Group) and the Welsh Schools. Although the English boys won the last match, on March 18 at Twickenham, they have a big leeway to make up, for the score now stands at Wales 55 wins, England 10, with five draws. *Geoff Abbott*

In a dramatic day at Newlands, New Zealand beat South Africa 9-8 in the second international match of their tour to level the series with two matches to go. It was a game that drew published recriminations, on either side; but there was never the remotest question that the All Blacks had earned victory in a cliff-hanger of a finish.

It was a matter of two New Zealand tries and a penalty goal to South Africa's goal and penalty, after the All Blacks had led 6-0 at half-time – and South Africa 8-6 into the last minute of normal time!

It was eight minutes from the end, in fact, that South Africa took the lead. Then, in a superb sustained burst of controlled attacking play, Lochore called his changes as he struck left and right constantly. It was a magnificent climax and an inspiring exhibition of captaincy. Without a shade of doubt, New Zealand earned their victory.

Wyllie was a marked success on the flank. The important Springbok half-back advantage of the first international was neutralised, and it was Laidlaw and Kirton this time who cracked the tactical whip.

Carwyn James, assistant manager of the British Lions in New Zealand next year, will be responsible for coaching the side, but he has no illusion about his task. Already he has started to 'pick the brains' of those with experience of New Zealand conditions, and, like manager Doug Smith, is prepared to burn the midnight oil in search of success.

James, a college lecturer, former international, ex-Parliamentary candidate and a Welsh Nationalist, was born at Cefneithin, a mining village near Carmarthen, in November, 1929. His father was a miner in the days when miners and schoolmasters were the very lifeblood of rugby in Wales.

James went to Gwendreath Grammar School in 1942 and remained there until 1948 before moving to University College, Aberystwyth, where he obtained an honours degree in languages.

His first game for the school first XV was as captain, and from 1946 to 1948 he played six times for the Welsh Secondary Schools, leading the side three times. He played for the village team during the war

Willie John McBride, a popular choice for the 1971 Lions tour to New Zealand.

years and appeared for Llanelli, while still at school, in the 1947-48 season.

James did his National Service in the Royal Navy in 1952-54 and appeared for the Services clubs. After that he had several Welsh trials before being capped at fly-half in December, 1957, against Australia. His other appearance for Wales was at centre, outside Cliff Morgan, against France in March, 1958.

While in the Services he had a year with London Welsh. He also appeared in three sevens finals at Twickenham for that club, and led the seven to victory in 1956.

He was a skilful and shrewd outside-half, while he could also play at full-back and centre, but his career was over-shadowed, internationally, by Cliff Morgan.

At club level he played many fine games for Llanelli, for whom he was a great favourite. The best players he appeared with were Terry Davies, Cyril Davies, Onllwyn Brace, Wynne Evans, R.H. Williams and Haydn Evans, while the best he met were Cliff Morgan, Roy Burnett, Peter Robbins and Peter Jones.
J B G Thomas

Much the happiest news in Midlands rugger as the new season got underway was that the breach between the Coventry and Rugby clubs had been healed, and that fixtures would begin again with a game on Rugby's ground on September 30.

The original cause of the matches between these traditional rivals being cancelled last season was the abrupt departure of England international Tim Dalton from Coundon Road to Webb Ellis Road, where he took over the captaincy of Rugby in the absence of injured Tim Cowell.

Coventry took such exception to the circumstances of Dalton's move that they decided to abandon fixtures with Rugby indefinitely. Fortunately, both sides have got together and decided to let bygones be bygones.

November 1970
Willie John McBride, whose second name is really James, was 30 last June 6, but that would not stop me taking him with the Lions to Australia and New Zealand next summer.

The formidable Irish lock-forward is still three years younger than was Alfred Roques, the pride of Cahors, when he won his first cap as a prop for France. That was against Australia in 1958, when he was 33. But the 'Rock' obtained 22 more caps after that. His last, against Scotland, came in 1963, not long before his 38th birthday. At that stage he was playing almost as well as ever.
Vivian Jenkins

For years, in various parts of the country, people have been grumbling about county rugby. It has been called a 'farce', a 'waste of time', a 'shambles'; yet there are plenty of men who believe it to be the lifeblood of the game.

No other subject in the rugby set-up has drawn such widely differing opinions, such controversy, or has reached such a complete impasse. If the Rugby Union was to offer a large reward to anyone who could produce a solution to satisfy everyone. I do not believe the prize would ever be won.

Ron Jacobs, that four-square England prop for eight years, and now representing East Midlands on the Rugby Union, is all for a regional system.

He told me: 'I think a regional championship would be better than the country one because the standard of play is bound to be higher. It would not necessarily cut out county matches; they could still be played, but I also think that somehow we have to reduce the number of games that take place in the early part of the season.'
Rupert Cherry

One reason why the thought of sponsored rugby makes me vaguely uneasy is that the whole idea of sponsorship is uneasily vague. What exactly is a sponsor? What can he do for rugby, and (just as relevant) what can rugby do for him? What's the difference between a sponsor, a patron, and advertiser and promoter?

There's a lot of muddled thinking about all this. One rugby writer commented recently: 'With commercial sponsors queueing up to give money to other sports, the clubs see no reason at all why rugby clubs should not accept their money as long as it is kept firmly under the control of the governing bodies.'

Now this begs a whole row of questions. For a start, no commercial sponsor in his right mind 'gives' money to any sport. What he does is finance a contest or competition (often putting up the prize money) in return for the publicity of having the shindig named after him, and usually getting a few fringe benefits in the form of advertising on the ground.

The key word is 'commercial'. Any businessman who allocates £50,000 from his advertising budget to sponsor a sporting contest expects to get his money back in publicity. If he has any other objective in mind, he may be a wonderful sportsman but he is a lousy businessman.
Derek Robinson

December 1970

The touring Fijians shocked the rugby world when they scored a brilliant and dramatic victory over the Barbarians at Gosforth in the sixth match of their tour, on October 24.

Britain's famous nomadic XV included 14 internationals – the 'odd man out' was D.L. Quinnell of Llanelli – but the Fijians, after a 3-3 half-time score, played the running game magnificently in the second half and triumphed by 29 points (four goals, three tries) to 9 (two tries, penalty goal).

Ismeli Batibasaga, their scrum-half, though not at his best, converted four tries

and scored one himself. This 22-year-old farmer, who stands 5 ft 7 ins and weighs 11 st 6 lb, has a long, speedy service and became a top-ranker in a matter of months.

In their games previous to the Gosforth match, the Fijians beat Devon and Cornwall at Exeter (17-3); lost to Gloucestershire and Somerset at Gloucester (13-25); drew with Midland Counties West at Coventry (16-16); beat North-West Counties at Broughton Park (11-6) and lost to North-East Counties at Bradford (6-14).

Fijian scrum-half Batibasaga gets his line moving during the visitors drawn game against Midland Counties West at Coventry.

Willie John McBride, of Ballymena and Ireland fame, has said he will not be available for the Lions' tour to Australia and New Zealand next year. McBride, a father of two, has to concentrate on his banking career, which is understandable, but it is a big loss to the Lions.

His strength and experience would have been a great help against the All Blacks. Also, he could have passed on to the new Lions the knowledge he has gained on previous tours.

He has been one of the great forwards, but no man is irreplaceable. McBride's withdrawal gives an opportunity for new men, like Derek Quinnell of Llanelli, to make a bid for selection.

Writing of the Lions' tour, I see the New Zealand papers have been making big play of a remark alleged to have been made by Dr Doug Smith, the touring team's manager-elect, at a Rugby Writers' Club luncheon in Fleet Street a month or two ago.

Dr Smith has been quoted by a New Zealand writer present at the luncheon as saying, with reference to his team's prospects: 'We will have enough backs to kick hell out of all the All Blacks'.

I was present at the luncheon, and my recollection of the phrase Dr Smith used was 'knock hell out of the All Blacks', which is very different; and he said it with a half-smile, which does not emerge in print.
Vivian Jenkins

Meanwhile, I have read with interest the scheme of Old Whitgiftian Martin Turner, as outlined by Rupert Cherry in last month's *Rugby World*. Mr Turner wants to divide the season into four separate periods, for clubs, counties, areas and internationals, with all matches being played on Saturdays.

This sounds fine in theory, but how would clubs such as Coventry and Northampton like having the second half of their season torn to shreds? Also, how would one fit in a national knock-out

competition for clubs? It is not as easy as it sounds.

On the whole, I think that England's rugby would benefit in the long run if the Rugby Union was to lay down that all county rugby should be played on Saturdays, or not at all. Then the Northern and South-Western Groups could carry on as now, and the others could make a choice.

It is one of the few ways that I can see of cutting down the number of matches a top man has to play in a season. And that, certainly, is highly necessary.
Vivian Jenkins

Australia will press for an increase in the value of a try from three to four points at the International Rugby Board meeting next March. They believe that the extra incentive for scoring tries would help to brighten play by putting a greater emphasis on attack.

There can hardly be any other motive in Australia's move, even though their own post-war teams have been notably lacking in goal-kickers through the selectors' habit of excluding players of talent in this department.

Had the value of the try been increased in the past five years, Australia would have had an even sorrier record in international matches than they have. The thrashing the British Isles gave them at Brisbane in 1966 would have been by 36-0, not 31-0.
Eddie Kann

A RUGBY QUIZ

compiled by NIGEL STARMER-SMITH

1. Which venue is the odd one out?

(a) Lord's; Oxford; Blackheath; Twickenham; Cambridge; The Oval; Queen's Club.

(b) Raeburn Place (Edinburgh); Headingley (Leeds); Athletic Ground (Richmond); Twickenham; Old Hampden Park (Glasgow); Kingsholm (Gloucester); Inverleith (Edinburgh); Murrayfield; the Oval; Fallowfield (Manchester); Powderhall (Edinburgh); Whalley Range (Manchester).

(c) Edge Hall Road; Pandy Park; Philiphaugh; the Gnoll; Central Park; Thomond Park; Blundellsands; Coundon Road; Donnybrook.

2. Which of the following 'Davies' did not play rugby for Wales (since 1970)?

Davies, T.G.R.; Davies, W.P.C.; Davies, W.G.; Davies, M.; Davies, T.M.; Davies, J.; Davies, J.D.; Davies, A.; Davies, P.T.; Davies, N.G.

3. Which of the following 'Smiths' did not play rugby for England?

Smith, J.V.; Smith, S.T.; Smith, S.R.; Smith, S.J.; Smith, I.S.

4. Fill the gaps in these sequences:

(a) Bath, Bath, Bath, Bath, Harlequins, —, Bath, Harlequins, Bath, Bath, Bath.

(b) Lancashire, —, Lancashire, —, Lancashire, Lancashire, Yorkshire.

(c) —, Swansea, Llanelli, Swansea.

(d) Llanelli, Neath, Neath, Llanelli, Llanelli, Llanelli, —.

(e) Kelso, Kelso, Melrose, —, Melrose, Melrose, Melrose.

5. In the context of the Rugby World Cup which two countries are the odd ones out?

Spain; Romania; Namibia; Ivory Coast; Fiji; Tonga; USA; Western Samoa; Zimbabwe; Canada; Italy.

6. Which nations came third and fourth in the 1987 and 1991 World Cups?

7. On which national rugby emblem will you see.

(a) a fern leaf; (b) an oak leaf; (c) a maple leaf; (d) a puma; (e) a palm tree by itself; (f) a palm tree plus five stars; (g) an ostrich; (h) the letters 'F.I.R.'?

8. Complete the following:

In major international fixtures
  Scotland have never beaten —.
  Wales have never beaten —.
  Ireland have never beaten —.

9. Which player holds the world record of most international match appearances for his country?

10. Which players have won the title Whitbread Rugby World Player of the Year (chosen from the four Home Countries) for the last five years?

(Answers on page 90)

WE'VE INVESTED TEN YEARS IN ENGLISH RUGBY

IT'S PAID OFF HANDSOMELY

This year, Save & Prosper will have been sponsoring English rugby for a whole decade.

And, all in all, it's been a very successful period.

Just as it has for many of the thousands of people who have invested money with us through our unit trusts, PEPs and other savings and investment schemes.

If you'd like to know more about how we could help you get the most from your money, just call us on our free Moneyline 0800 282 101.

THE SAVE & PROSPER INTERNATIONALS

12 NOVEMBER 1994	ENGLAND v ROMANIA
10 DECEMBER 1994	ENGLAND v CANADA
4 FEBRUARY 1995	ENGLAND v FRANCE
18 MARCH 1995	ENGLAND v SCOTLAND

PLUS

13 MAY 1995 SAVE & PROSPER MIDDLESEX SEVENS

© R.F.U. 1982

SAVE & PROSPER

■ THE INVESTMENT HOUSE ■
SPONSORS OF ENGLISH RUGBY

UNIT TRUSTS • PEPS • PENSIONS • SCHOOL FEES PLANS • BANKING SERVICES

SAVE & PROSPER GROUP LTD IS A MEMBER OF IMRO AND LAUTRO

REVIEW OF THE SEASON
1993-94

MEDIOCRITY AND MAGNIFICENCE
The 1994 Five Nations Championship

by BILL McLAREN

The 1994 Five Nations Championship will not go into rugby lore as one of the most enjoyable competitions. Far from it. In spectacle, try-scoring, continuity and daring it fell far short of essential standards and pointed again to the need for legislation that will offer incentives to coaches and players to seek a style of genuine total rugby embracing far more frequent spread of play to the wings.

Yet despite the lack of flowing passages and rippling back-division attacks, the game, at its highest echelon, could hardly have been more popular, with capacity audiences at every international, tickets thus hard to come by and, as one example, a staggering £1.4 million being taken in gate receipts at the England v Ireland match at Twickenham. There is, of course, a strong element of national pride, an all-embracing obsession with winning almost at whatever cost, intense competitiveness and, of course, that desire on the part of the paying spectator to be there on the day which makes the hospitality package so popular, all of which helps to swell the demand for tickets. How long this will last, as well as the attractiveness of the Rugby Union game to sponsors, is open to question, especially if the actual playing of the game at the very top level does not take into account the requirement to entertain those big crowds who have to fork out quite large sums for the so-called privilege of just being there.

The 1994 campaign also underlined that the gulf between the strong and the weaker is not now so wide, for it encompassed some unexpected results, not least the re-emergence of Wales as a potent force and as winners of the Championship on points differential. There was, too, that shattering defeat of England at Twickenham by an Irish side which scored the only try of the match through the electric Simon Geoghegan and which demonstrated that defensively they are now much better organised. Although Scotland ended up with the wooden spoon, they still hauled themselves up from the disasters of conceding ten tries in catastrophic defeats by New Zealand (15-51) and Wales (6-29) to give the might of England a torrid time at Murrayfield before going down 14-15 to one of the great pressure penalty goals of all time – that by Jonathan Callard, with the last kick of the game.

An uncertain start for England. Scotland's Gary Armstrong (above) touches down for a 'try' that was disallowed before England edged home by a single point at Murrayfield. Simon Geoghegan (left) outpaces Tony Underwood to score Ireland's winning try at Twickenham.

Neil Jenkins listens over his shoulder to Ieuan Evans' half-time team talk at Lansdowne Road.

There was a touch of anti-climax about the Welsh success when they were presented with the Championship trophy after they had lost 8-15 to England at Twickenham on the closing day. Nonetheless, it was a notable feat for the Welsh to take the title with three wins out of four because, prior to the start of the Championship, all had been sunk in deep dejection in the valleys after Wales had suffered one of their most humiliating defeats when Canada beat them 26-24 at Cardiff in November. There were suggestions that the positions of manager Robert Norster and coach Alan Davies were in danger; yet those two effected a remarkable transformation in attitude and effort so that Wales, though never quite productive enough in line-out play, were characteristically competitive and aggressive elsewhere. What is more, they reached out so successfully for their traditional style of swift ball transference among their backs as to register seven Championship tries, a mark bettered only by France with nine. Wales, indeed, scored more tries in the 1994 Championship than in the previous two combined, and it was an indication of their playing pattern that six of their seven tries were by their backs, five by their wings.

It was, however, something of an indictment of the law-makers, coaches and players that the ten Championship games spawned only 20 tries – the same as in 1993 – compared to 36 in 1991 and 34 in 1992.

Wales had an opening home match against Scotland which was billed by the media as 'a wooden spoon decider' because England and France had already been installed as favourites for the title. Wales did not play like wooden spoonists. In seeping rain, they scored three cracking tries and had a bonus in the clear signs that Neil Jenkins was developing into a stand-off with vision and authority and sound option choice, an impression confirmed in subsequent games, as was his worth as match-winning points-scorer. He was responsible for 48 of Wales' 78 points.

The Welsh had their luck. They would have lost in Dublin had not the usually reliable Eric Elwood, having already potted five penalty goals, struck a match-winning sitter penalty against a post. Wales won 17-15, the only try by Neil Jenkins showing the value of quickly recycled breakdown ball. The Welsh thus had won two Championship games in a row for the first time since 1988. They would also have lost to France in Cardiff but Thierry Lacroix missed seven goal-kicks and Alain Penaud a dropped goal. The French revived from 3-17 down to 15-17 with tries by Olivier Roumat and the durable Philippe Sella but Wales, having been inspired by a remarkable individualist try by 21-year-old Scott Quinnell, son of the former British Lions forward, Derek, kept fingers in the dyke for a famous victory by 24-15. The newcomer Quinnell was to make quite an impact upon Welsh success although, in the England game, he found, as had others before him, that Dean Richards is a hard man to outpoint.

That England v Wales game at Twickenham actually proved the most attractive in the Championship. England, led on by Brian Moore to mark his 50th cap, ended 438 minutes of tryless action with a glorious move involving Dewi Morris, Will Carling, Rob Andrew with a miss pass, and Philip de Glanville, who then sent Rory Underwood streaking home. England won 15-8 but they had needed a clear 16-point margin to snatch the Championship on points differential. They did deny Wales a Grand Slam whilst finding a resourceful and adventurous full-back in Ian Hunter.

England, however, were disappointing in that they had the personnel to paint a broad canvas but remained tactically predictable and reluctant to let their hair down in handling flow. They were fortunate to beat Scotland, who scored the only try through Rob Wainwright in a tight contest in which the scoring sequence was (Scotland first): 0-3; 5-3; 8-3; 8-6; 8-9; 11-9; 11-12; 14-12; 14-15. For Scotland, who had lost Craig Chalmers (cheekbone) and pack leader Iain Morrison (leg fracture) in the Welsh match, it was a case of elation to despair as Callard potted his match-winning fifth penalty goal.

Scott Quinnell sets Wales on their way to a 24-15 win over France in Cardiff.

Olivier Roumat (above) scores the only try of the match between England and France in Paris and Rory Underwood (above right) escapes Ieuan Evans' tackle to score England's first try of the Championship in their last game against Wales at Twickenham.

Noel Murphy attributed Ireland's 13-12 win at Twickenham to the fact that 'England played just as we expected them to'. There was also a brilliant Geoghegan try from a London Irish move in which feint runs were made by full-back and centre as the blind-side wing intruded at pace. It was Ireland's first win at Twickenham since 1982 and England's first Championship defeat at home since Wales beat them 11-3 in 1988.

England's most praiseworthy performance was in Paris, where they won 18-14, their seventh consecutive triumph over France. That was a day to remember for Rob Andrew, whose kicking from hand was searchingly accurate and who scored all his side's points with five penalty goals and a dropped goal – his 16th for England, a Northern Hemisphere record. England's style wasn't pretty but their defence and discipline were rock-solid, especially when Lacroix twice brought France to within a point. One post-match comment by the French coach, Pierre Berbizier, was: 'England's style is efficient but I hope rugby will be the winner when they play Wales.'

The French always looked the most capable of stitching together passages of quickfire handling and they came to the boil early with four tries in launching their defence of the title with a 35-15 home margin against Ireland, who battled bravely but whose forwards tired against stronger opponents so that the late tries by Philippe Saint-André and Olivier Merle gave the winning margin a somewhat artificial appearance. The French, however, failed to bring scoring chances to fruition against Wales and England and so were persuaded to introduce three new caps against Scotland for a 20-12 win, their first at Murrayfield since 1978. In that match the Hastings brothers, Gavin and Scott, reached the magic milestone of 50 caps together, but it was France who produced perhaps the try of the Championship when their two big loose forwards, Abdel Benazzi and Philippe Benetton, made dents off a scrummage and created sweet ruck ball from which Lacroix's miss pass enabled the new centre cap, Yann Delaigue, to make a searing break. He followed up with a perfect chip ahead for full-back Jean-Luc Sadourny to score. So after a match which contained 49 line-outs and just 15 scrummages, France were left to rue what might have been and Scotland with the wooden spoon.

After both England's home games in the Championship their opponents took a bow. Ireland (below) savoured a rare win at Twickenham and Wales (above) received the Five Nations trophy, despite losing their final game.

The Irish held firmly to a policy of punt and pack, Elwood's educated boot being the major influence. As for Scotland, their one point stemmed from that 6-6 draw in Dublin when they gave a memorable display of rucking against the elements in the first half but failed to harness the stiff wind after the break, although their new loose forward find, Peter Walton of Northampton, came within inches of a late try. That match was notable for the devastating return of Gary Armstrong to the international fold after his self-imposed exile from scrum-half duty. He was immense and there was some satisfaction for the Scots also in the emergence as players with potential of Gregor Townsend, with his sizzling acceleration; Alan Sharp, who shored up the loose-head berth; Shade Munro, much more effective as front jumper, and Walton, big and bruising.

The Championship, however, lacked consistent sparkle. As David Hands wrote in *The Times*, it proved 'an addictive mixture of mediocrity and magnificence'. It was a campaign dominated by error and claustrophobic defence rather than by skilled construction. And as Gerald Davies wrote, also in *The Times*: 'The prize and the statistics are becoming more important than the game's brilliance.'

Much blame was placed at the door of the turnover law leading to midfield defences being cluttered by detached forwards, but the plain fact is that far too many reasonable opportunities of handling attack were ignored in preference for further bouts of aerial ping-pong.

ANSWERS

to A Rugby Quiz (on page 81)

1. (a) Lord's: all the other locations have hosted the Oxford v Cambridge Varsity Match.
(b) Kingsholm: all the other venues have staged the England v Scotland international match.
(c) Central Park, the home of Wigan Rugby League club: all the others are Rugby Union club venues.
2. Davies, W.P.C. was an England international (Harlequins and England, 1953-58). The others played for Wales in recent years.
3. Smith, I.S. played for Scotland and was an outstanding wing threequarter, 1924-1933.
4. (a) Bath: Pilkington Cup winners 1989.
(b) Durham and Cornwall: county champions 1989 and 1991.
(c) Neath: Heineken League winners 1991.
(d) Cardiff: SWALEC Welsh Cup winners 1994.
(e) Boroughmuir: McEwan's Scottish League winners 1991.
5. Spain and Namibia have yet to qualify for the final rounds of a Rugby World Cup – Ivory Coast have qualified for the 1995 finals.
6. 1987: 3rd Wales, 4th Australia.
1991: 3rd New Zealand, 4th Scotland.
7. (a) New Zealand; (b) Romania; (c) Canada; (d) Argentina; (e) Fiji; (f) Western Samoa; (g) Australia (part of the larger crest);(h) Italy.
8. Scotland have never beaten New Zealand.
Wales have never beaten South Africa.
Ireland have never beaten New Zealand.
9. Philippe Sella: 101 appearances for France so far
(up to 2 September 1994)
10. 1990 Brian Moore; 1991 Dean Richards; 1992 Will Carling;
1993 Ieuan Evans; 1994 Ben Clarke.

Key Players for 1994-95

England

Rory Underwood

Tim Rodber

First capped in 1984, Rory has been a regular member of the team ever since and he is now not only England's most-capped player – 67 at the start of this season – but also the record try-scorer with 36. Furthermore, when he scored five tries against Fiji in 1989, he equalled the record in one match for an English international set by Dan Lambert in 1907.

He is one of only three members of the current England side who has played in both the 1987 and 1991 World Cups and also had the distinction of playing in all three Tests in the last two British Lions tours, to Australia in 1989 and to New Zealand in 1993. He has electrifying pace, a tremendous swerve and an uncanny knack of being able to beat people in a very confined space. He used all these skills plus a natural vision for the game to score a remarkable try against Ireland in Dublin to clinch the Triple Crown in 1991. He also scored an equally memorable try for the British Lions in their great victory in the Second Test in Wellington in 1993, when he used his searing acceleration to leave the All Blacks flat-footed in a wonderful sprint to the line. After their recent try famine, he is just the player to set the English back division alight. He retired briefly after the publication of his autobiography, *Flying Wing,* in 1992, but, to England's delight, he soon changed his mind and will add a wealth of experience to their World Cup challenge.

Every year players seem to get bigger and heavier and the English loose forward combination in the famous victory over New Zealand at Twickenham last season played a significant part in a remarkable performance. Tim Rodber added his 6 foot 6 and 16-stone bulk to that of Dean Richards (6 foot 4 and 17 stone) and Ben Clarke (6 foot 6 and 16 stone). It is hardly surprising that with these three giants at the back and the luxury of being able to perm any two locks from Bayfield, Johnson and Redman, England are a formidable force at the line-out and a very difficult side to outscrummage. Tim Rodber has made excellent progress since playing for England Under-21s in 1990, going on to win two caps in 1992 against Scotland and Ireland. He showed his outstanding footballing skills when he helped England win the first-ever World Sevens at Murrayfield in 1993 and topped a great year by playing in the win over the All Blacks. He is good with the ball in his hands and is also a good support player. Some critics feel the current English back row is unbalanced because all three players probably feel their best position is at number 8, but Ben Clarke has proved he has enough pace to play at open-side flanker and Tim Rodber has shown he is just as good in defence as he is in attack. The efforts of Rodber and his back-row colleagues will go a long way to determining England's record this season.

FRANCE

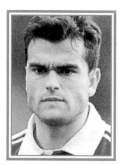

ALAIN PENAUD

ABDELATIF BENAZZI

After a very promising schools career in which he helped French Schools beat England, Wales and Scotland in 1987, Penaud soon made an impact at club level in France as an exciting attacking fly-half with outstanding kicking ability. By the age of 21 he had been selected to play for France A and he went on to win his first full cap against Wales in Cardiff in 1992. He played in all the matches in the Five Nations Championship that year, and in the Test series against Argentina and South Africa. However, just when it looked as if he had established himself in the side, he was replaced in 1993 by Didier Camberabero. Last season he returned to the team and his open style of play will be important in helping France recapture their great threequarter play, which has been missing in recent internationals. Penaud has a good eye for a gap and is also quick to create space for his back division. He is not yet quite as effective as Camberabero as a tactical kicker, but he has all the necessary skills and with experience he could be one of the best French fly-halves since the days of Jean-Pierre Romeu in the mid-70s.

Many of France's recent problems in can be overcome with new, inspired direction at fly-half and Penaud is the ideal player for this crucial task. The French pack is not as formidable as it was and their success in this year's Championship and the World Cup will depend a lot on the play of Penaud.

It is interesting to note that after Morocco did so well in the World Cup qualifying group in Africa, just failing to reach the final 16 teams, their most famous international player, Benazzi, has become the most important forward in the French side. He played for Morocco in the qualifying rounds of the 1991 World Cup but, by then, he was already living and playing in France. He moved from Cahors, a Second Division club, to First Division Agen, and won his first cap for France against Australia in 1990. It was not the great occasion he had anticipated because he was sent off early in the first half, but he played the remaining Tests on that tour and in both Tests later that year in France against the All Blacks. He played at flanker against Australia and at lock against New Zealand, but eventually was chosen in his favourite position of number 8 in his first Five Nations match, against England in 1991. He is now one of the most experienced forwards in the current French team and with his great versatility he is guaranteed to be a key member of the pack for the next few seasons. He is a very useful jumper at the back of the line-out (he's 6 foot 6), a strong scrummager and, most important of all, he is outstanding in the open. He is a solid, defensive player but he is at his best on the attack, especially when he has Laurent Cabannes with him in the back row. It seems France have the makings of a good pack built around Benazzi.

IRELAND

CONOR O'SHEA

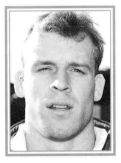

BRIAN ROBINSON

Ireland have found full-back a real problem position in the last two years and in a game of musical chairs, when the music has stopped they have, on varying occasions, turned to Murphy, Staples, Wilkinson, Clarke and, most recently, 23-year-old Conor O'Shea. He graduated in the now accepted way by playing two seasons in the Irish Under-21 side when he was a student at University College, Dublin before joining Lansdowne, where he won provincial honours with Leinster. In 1993 he went with the Irish Development squad on their tour to Southern Africa and made a very favourable impression, scoring six tries in four matches. He had a splendid season with Leinster and won his first full cap against Romania before going on to play in all the Five Nations games. He played very well in the tremendous Irish victory over England at Twickenham and certainly has the ability to establish himself in the side. At 6 foot 2 and over 14 stone he is a big, strong runner in attack and a very solid defensive player. So far he has had limited opportunities to show his flair for attack because the Irish back division has not been a particularly well co-ordinated or fluent unit, but his chance will surely come and he could be just the player to kick-start this season's Irish recovery.

Even in their most difficult years, when victories have not been all that common, the Irish have always been able to produce a decent, really competitive, pack with a few outstanding forwards. One such player is Brian Robinson, who has been their key man in the back row. Just as Popplewell, Kingston and Clohessy make a mighty solid and effective front row, so the rest of the pack has been built round the skills of Brian Robinson. After playing for Ireland B and Ireland Under-25s, he won his first full cap against France in 1991 and has been a regular member of the side for the past four years. He is usually a number 8, but he has also won caps at blind-side flanker. A good player with the ball in his hands, he has scored six tries in international rugby, which puts him right up at the top of Irish try-scoring list alongside Simon Geoghegan, although less charitable critics may be quick to point out that four of his six tries were scored during the World Cup match in 1991 against Zimbabwe. He is a good defensive player and is quick around the field in support, considering he is 6 foot 4 and over 15 stone. In recent matches he has been Ireland's main ball-winner at the back of the line-out and if Ireland are to recover from their disappointing season in 1994, which culminated in their unsuccessful tour to Australia, they will look to Robinson to lead the way.

SCOTLAND

GREGOR TOWNSEND

KENNY MILNE

The Scots have been very fortunate in having two great pairs of half-backs in the last few years. John Rutherford and Roy Laidlaw were replaced by Craig Chalmers and Gary Armstrong and now Chalmers has given way at fly-half to Gregor Townsend. He is one of the most exciting talents to emerge in British rugby in the 1990s as he has tremendous speed off the mark, he is a very elusive runner with a great eye for a gap and he has shown he can rip the best-organised defence to shreds. He is the sort of jinking fly-half more readily seen in Wales in the past, and although he needs to add a little more discipline to his play at international level there is no doubt he will be a major influence on Scotland's fortunes in the build-up to the 1995 World Cup. Amazingly, he is still only 21 years old and is bound to be an even better player with more experience. He played for Scotland B against France B in 1992 when he was only 18 and then in four matches for Scotland A before winning his first cap, when he came on as a replacement against England in 1993. He had an outstanding tour with Scotland to Australia in 1992, playing in four of the games and scoring two tries and two dropped goals. His dropped goal in the last minute of the Calcutta Cup game last season looked to have won the game for Scotland before Callard's injury-time penalty stole it for England, but he will surely help restore Scotland's fortunes in the near future.

Along with Paul Burnell, Kenny Milne is the most experienced Scottish forward in the current team with 30 caps and one British Lions tour behind him. He is a part of a remarkable sporting family: both his brothers have played international rugby in the front row for Scotland in the past few years. Iain won 44 caps at tight-head prop, while David played once in 1991. Kenny won his first cap against Wales in 1989 and was a key member of Scotland's Grand Slam-winning team in 1990. He is an accurate thrower-in at the line-out, which is such an important part of a hooker's job nowadays, and he has enjoyed a big reputation as a player of great skill in the open. Apart from being acknowledged for his speed around the pitch, he is a past master at securing the ball in the rucks and mauls and has also put in more than his fair share of tackles in broken play. He is a good support player and has been rewarded for his efforts with three tries for Scotland. He won selection for the British Lions tour to New Zealand in 1993 and played in the First Test. This could well be his last season of international rugby and he is bound to be an important focal point for the Scottish forward effort as they endeavour to have a much better season in the Five Nations and to make a big impact in the World Cup in South Africa next summer.

WALES

NEIL JENKINS

SCOTT QUINNELL

After a succession of great Welsh fly-halves in the past 25 years, spearheaded by Barry John, Phil Bennett and Jonathan Davies, the supply dried up when Davies went to Rugby League in 1988. Now another prolific points-scorer has emerged to bring pride once again to the number 10 jersey in Neil Jenkins, a young player with an exciting future. It has to be said that he is in a very different mould from those other brilliant fly-halves who guided Wales to glory in the past, but he is an extremely steady, consistent player who has a solid defence, a tremendous boot on him and who has the ability to bring out the best in those around him by choosing the right time to unleash the back division. What is more, he is a first-class goal-kicker with a remarkable record, having raced well past 200 points in international rugby in just four years. He has already demonstrated his versatility by playing half a dozen internationals in the centre and one at full-back before establishing himself in 1994 as the automatic choice at fly-half. He was one of the most influential figures in the Welsh resurgence last season and played a leading part in Wales' victory in the Five Nations Championship. Barring injury, he looks certain, at the incredibly young age of 23, to become Wales' highest points-scorer, because at the start of this season, in which he is likely to play up to a dozen internationals, he is already within striking distance of Paul Thorburn's record of 304 points.

Every so often a new player explodes on to the international scene with such force that he catches all the headlines and everyone's imagination. Ben Clarke did it for England two years ago and Scott Quinnell's first season of international rugby was every bit as dramatic. Built in the same proportions as his father, Wales and British Lions forward Derek Quinnell, Scott is 6 foot 4 and around 17 stone, and it is no surprise that he made his mark as a schoolboy. He won Welsh caps for the Schools, the Under-19 and then the Under-21 sides before representing Wales A. He won his first full cap when he was selected to play against Canada in November 1993, and although Wales lost, he showed his outstanding potential. He had an excellent game against Scotland in January 1994 and played a major role in the victory over Ireland in Dublin. There is no doubt his best moment came when he scored a spectacular try against France in a storming run, leaving half the French team trailing in his wake. It was the most talked-about try of the year and when you consider that he begins this new season as an established international and is still only 21 years of age, it is easy to appreciate how excited they are in Wales that they have unearthed a great player for the 90s. He is dynamic in attack, good at the line-out, strong in defence and he is likely to be the apex of the Welsh forward thrust for many years to come.

THE CLUB SCENE

NO ONE'S EVER SATISFIED!
by Bill Mitchell

So, the top clubs had the kind of competition they wanted, but as we go to press there are plenty of people who are far from satisfied that a perfect arrangement has been reached even though each side in the top four Courage Leagues now meets its opponents twice in a season, home and away.

Apparently the pressures on the players are too great, a point which was well demonstrated by the patchy form of England during the 1994 tour to South Africa, which had only one good moment (that superb First Test win in Pretoria) and several bad ones.

Jack Rowell, the new England supremo, has taken it all to heart and feels, undoubtedly correctly, that England's hopes of winning the World Cup in 1995 in South Africa will only be realistic if the selected players have no matches to play in April 1995 . This will definitely not suit several senior clubs, among them his old friends from Bath, who could be asked to rest half their team during a vital period of the season.

Leicester flankers Wells and Back give support to Dean Richards in Leicester's win over Bath early last season.

But no one should be surprised by all this. Under the old structure, clubs played a dozen League matches and that was probably too many. Now they have another six competitive games added to their burdens and it is definitely too much. The size of the new Leagues was determined for the benefit of club treasurers and sponsors – certainly not for the long-term good of the England team – and it is a problem that will return every time there is a World Cup and probably on other occasions. So the Leagues will have to be made even smaller – perhaps five leagues of eight clubs each with Leagues 5 North and South becoming effective sixth divisions?

Nonetheless, there was a good League programme last season, although the top division did not really share in that excitement since the destination of the title and the fates of the teams at the foot of the table were decided long before the final day. Bath, as expected, retained their

The end of an era. Twickenham's famous West Stand is demolished to begin the final phase of the rebuilding of rugby's headquarters.

Ian Hunter makes
a break for
England at
Twickenham,
leaving Welsh
backs Mike Rayer
(left) and Ieuan
Evans in disarray.

Scotland's Alan Sharp stays on his feet despite the efforts of Argentinian Pedro Sporleder. Moving in to help are (left to right) Scots McKenzie, Smith, Walton, Reed and Burnell.

Leicester scrum-half Aadel Kardooni encourages his forwards to fetch the ball for him during the game against Bath which Leicester won 9-6 at Welford Road.

CONNECTIONS

well as the best connections around Asia and also on to 15 cities in

Mike Hall (with the ball) has support from Scott Quinnell (left) and Mike Rayer at Twickenham where, despite their defeat, Wales eventually secured the 1994 Five Nations Championship.

A rural setting for
Dunvant's home
ground. The 'new
boys' at the top
level in Wales
were successful in
staying up after
their first season
in Division 1 of
the Heieneken
Leagues.

Swansea captain
Stuart Davies lifts
the Heineken
League trophy
after a decisive
32-3 win over
Aberavon.

WE ALSO HAVE A PASSION FOR FOOTSIE

We know our way around the FT-SE index and the stock market like others know their way around the rugby pitch. In fact, in the investment field, few are a match for Save & Prosper.

To find out how Save & Prosper can help with your savings and investment plans, call us free on 0800 282 101.

UNIT TRUSTS • PEPS • PENSIONS • SCHOOL FEES PLANS • BANKING SERVICES
SAVE & PROSPER GROUP LTD IS A MEMBER OF IMRO AND LAUTRO

title with a six-point margin over Leicester, who were their only conquerors during the campaign with a narrow early-season victory at Welford Road.

The two clubs also met in a thoroughly shoddy Pilkington Cup final at Twickenham, which Bath also won (21-9), and it in no way enhanced the prestige of the Whitbread Rugby World Club of the Year Award that the two finalists were on the shortlist with Melrose, who would have been worthy winners instead of the West Country side.

The relegation issue was also settled early and the two to take the drop were London Irish, who were beset by internal bickering, and Newcastle Gosforth, who played bravely but were just not good enough. They are replaced

Recurring injury finally persuaded Stuart Barnes to hang up his boots, but he will still be very much a part of the club scene as host of Sky Sports new live coverage of club rugby.

at the top by Sale and West Hartlepool after a thrilling race which ended with the two teams meeting on the final day of the season in the north-east. Each side went into the game with the same number of match points and the subsequent draw left Sale champions with a vastly superior points difference.

Neither club was challenged for promotion in the latter stages of the season, but a shock defeat for West at London Scottish in the penultimate match not only gave Scottish a salvation lifeline, but also deprived the northern club of the Second Division title.

The Scots went on to win at Saracens in their last game and their escape left Rugby (for a second successive season) and Otley going down with Coventry and Fylde as their replacements from Division 3, which enjoyed an exciting battle for the top honours. Bedford, Blackheath and Rosslyn Park all had their moments and might with luck have gone up.

Again the trapdoor places from Division 3 were decided early with Havant and Redruth well adrift and their successors, Clifton and Harrogate, were well clear of their two challengers long before lights out. Clifton were Division 4 champions by four clear points from the Yorkshire club and in the process were the only unbeaten club in the National Leagues, also providing as bonuses the leading League points-scorer, fly-half Simon Hogg, and top try-scorer John Phillips.

It was sad to see such a famous club as Sheffield joining brave Sudbury at the foot of Division 4, which means 5 North rugby for them next season, but how refreshing it is also to see such names as Rotherham and Reading rise even higher in the pecking order as 5 North and 5 South champions respectively.

Equally thrilling is the prospect of having such clubs as Wharfedale, Barker's Butts, Henley and Barking joining the senior ranks. Any set of competitions which can give a chance in the big time to ambitious teams can only be good, and it will be interesting to see whether Gloucester Old Boys, who have been promoted six seasons in seven, can go one further and rise from South-West 1 to senior status.

Elsewhere, Twickenham had only one stand to complete before it will become just about the best stadium there is, and there was a moment to savour in November 1993, when the All Blacks – 51-15 winners a week earlier against Scotland at Murrayfield – were beaten 15-9 by England's superb defensive performance, Jonathan Callard enjoying a fine debut. They never quite rose to those heights again and even lost at home to Ireland, but it proved that the visitors were not unbeatable. The team did have a fine win in Paris and broke their tries drought in the final game against Wales at headquarters, but not enough points were scored to stop the trophy from going to the Principality.

Oxford won a dull Varsity Match at Twickenham against an inexperienced Cambridge, whose side will benefit from having most of the same players back again in 1994 along with some well-known recruits. It is therefore reasonable to expect that the recent vast improvement in the Oxbridge standards will be maintained after this brief hiccup. With players like Canada's Gareth Rees on show there is plenty of class available.

Two new names appeared in the UAU final, in which Northumbria University (a former polytechnic) beat West London Institute by 13-9 in a scrappy match, while St Mary's regained an ever-shrinking Hospitals Cup with a narrow 19-18 win over holders Charing Cross-Westminster amidst plenty of excitement.

Twickenham also saw the thrilling final of the new Pilkington Shield competition in which Malvern just beat Old Hamptonians by 8-6. Many felt that if they had returned home immediately after that match they would have been spared the poor fare offered by Bath and Leicester later that afternoon.

Headquarters also saw some fine services matches, with the RAF retaining their crown after just beating off the challenge of the Army, while the County Championship final was an all north-east affair, in which Yorkshire easily beat Durham, nobly aided by 'the try of the season' from the admirable veteran wing Mike Harrison. With the South-West winning the divisional honours in a New Year decider against London (both sides were at virtual half-strength), the famous ground was not without its moments.

In fact, Bath provided the last word there by fielding a shadow seven and taking the Middlesex honours from gallant Orrell, who would have a justified case for referring the matter to the Commission for Fair Trading or the Monopolies Commission as the club from the Rec stole yet another trophy.

The new season will start without some well-known faces. Geoff Cooke, after seven fine years in charge, gave up the England manager's job in March and only time will tell just how good an organising effort he put in. Bath will start the new season without the retired Gareth Chilcott and Stuart Barnes, and others are probably only waiting for the completion of the World Cup before stepping out of the limelight. Where will Brian Moore, Rob Andrew, Rory Underwood and other veterans, for example, be in 1995-96?

By then the game, which is already professional in everything but name, could possibly become honest and meet the insurmountable problem by declaring every person to be a 'player'. If this happens, only a small percentage of players will actually be professionals, but it would save everyone a lot of bother and could in the end enhance the prestige of Rugby Union. It would certainly improve the game's integrity.

A last home appearance for Gareth Chilcott. Surrounded by Bath colleagues he waves goodbye to supporters at the Recreation Ground after the Courage League match against Newcastle Gosforth.

INCONSISTENCY REIGNS
by Sean Diffley

Even if two consecutive wins over England augmented the larder nicely, Ireland are not too optimistic about the immediate future – the Five Nations Championship this winter and the World Cup the following summer. This means that Irish rugby is in its usual parlous state, often capable of reaching the very heights, but too often seemingly dedicated to scraping the barrel. Inconsistency generally reigns, a state which can vary from the irritating to the mildly amusing, depending on from which seat you view the proceedings.

The truth is, of course, that Irish rugby is fated to play ducks and drakes with victories and defeats for the simple, basic reason that it is a minor sport on the green and misty isle, with only about 20,000 participants. Thus it plays a secondary role to Jack Charlton's footballers and to Gaelic football in the number of its adherents.

Yet it works hard to keep in touch with the big boys. For a start, the IRFU is a wealthy organisation and once again at the annual meeting of the Irish Rugby Football Union last June, the treasurer was able to announce an operating surplus for the year of well over £1 million, plus more than £14 million on deposit. There is adequate sponsorship at all levels, from support for clubs to the Irish Permanent Building Society, which neatly and unfussily slipped in to take over from Digital Equipment as the sponsors of the internationals at Lansdowne Road, a national ground which now boasts first-class floodlighting as well as all the other necessary amenities.

Down the years the Irish have supplied more than their fair share of top-class players, the Kyles, Gibsons, O'Reillys, McBrides, Campbells and Wards. The difficulty is that Ireland is usually gifted with only one or two real 'sparklers' amidst their rough diamonds. The pool is too small to really cut a dash all the time.

And the way the game is developing does not suit the Irish all that well. Now it's a game based more and more on the forwards, who must be big men, tall basketball players, minimum height 6 foot 6 at the line-outs, 17 stone at least for the scrums and rucks. Ireland lacks men of such physical proportions and no matter how brave and committed they are – as against Australia in the quarter-final of the World Cup, or England over the past two seasons – such wins will only underline the inconsistency.

In all these circumstances, then, one is reminded of the W. C. Fields adage: 'If at first you don't succeed, try, try again. Then quit. No use being a damn fool about it.'

Well, the Irish, apparently, are determined to continue to be 'damn fools', broadening the number of technical staff at IRFU headquarters at Lansdowne Road, organising the structures from schools upwards, and this year concentrating for the fifth season since it was inaugurated on the highly successful All-Ireland League, sponsored by the Insurance Corporation company. The Irish Schools have been doing particularly well, achieving a couple of 'triple crowns' in recent seasons and always being capable of performing well against the best. The Under-21 sides have also had excellent returns.

But it is the All-Ireland League which has captured the imagination. Ireland was the last of the major rugby nations to institute a national club trophy and it is accepted that this hard-nosed competition will gradually hone the edges of the country's leading players. For too long the domestic game was afflicted with meaningless friendlies. Not any longer, and nowhere has the enthusiasm been greater than in Munster. All four All-Ireland competitions have been won – and won fairly convincingly – by Munster clubs, starting off with Cork Constitution, in the inaugural year of 1991, followed by Garryowen, then Young Munster and last season by Garryowen for the second time. Morever the runners-up in each season have also been Munster clubs.

Nick Popplewell, who has decided to play his club rugby in England.

So, as we enter the fifth season of the Insurance Corporation All-Ireland League, it very much behoves Ulster, Leinster and Connacht to do something about this one-way traffic. There has not been a lot of movement of players entering this new season of 1994-95. The most dramatic is the decision of Nick Popplewell to join Wasps. Greystones also

Brian Rigney will be winning line-out ball for Shannon in future.

lose another international in lock Brian Rigney, who has gone to Shannon.

There is some good young talent about, like the flying Blackrock College wing Nial Woods, his club-mate at fly-half, Alan McGowan, and the very highly rated – by no less a judge than Australian coach Bob Dwyer – hardy Garryowen hooker Keith Wood. Keith is a son of the late Gordon Wood, Lions and Ireland prop. The task of Ireland coach Gerry Murphy and manager Noel 'Noisy' Murphy will be to blend in this lot of young talent with the experienced players. And with the World Cup only months away, time is of the essence.

Looming over this new domestic season will be the memories of the summer's trials and tribulations on the tour of Australia: two Test defeats (33-13 and 33-18) and only a couple of wins over meagre provincial opposition. What so clearly emerged was that while the forwards, among them Wood, Clohessy, Francis and a new discovery, David Corkery from Cork Constitution, did all right, the situation among the backs was pretty awful. The only attacking idea behind the scrum seemed to be a hefty kick to the wing for Simon Geoghegan to chase. Otherwise the standards of cohesive play seemed totally beyond the midfield backs. On the firm surfaces of Australia they hadn't an attacking clue. On the firm World Cup surfaces of South Africa they will fare just as badly unless revolutionary changes are made. Ireland needs half-backs and centres.

From Gerry Murphy the call goes out, loud and desperate. Murphy makes it clear that he felt let down by his players in Australia.

A newish idea this season is that manager and coach will meet the provincial coaches and as many club coaches as they can to form as close a liaison as possible. That has not happened in the past as provincial coaching staff – never mind clubs – felt they had never been noticed, let alone spoken to, by some of Ireland's former management personnel.

We can but hope that this is another step in the right direction.

MASTERFUL MELROSE JOIN THE ELITE
by Bill McLaren

The Scottish club game in 1993-94 once again was dominated by Melrose, who now have taken on a mantle similar to that carried by Bath in England and Swansea and Llanelli in Wales.

Not only have Melrose captured the McEwan's Division 1 title for the fourth time in the past five years and also carried off the Border Championship for the fifth time in a row, a feat previously achieved only by Hawick, but they surely will be the team to beat in 1994-95 – provided that the lure of the English club game does not prove too attractive to some of their most experienced personnel. Certainly there is an ocean of mileage in the current Melrose side, whose average age, in winning the title, was 23. The Greenyards club proved worthy champions not only in the quality of their performances, which embraced the 15-man game more often than their critics would admit, but because they were capable of adapting their style to suit specific demands and conditions.

They were resilient too. As reigning champions they were shocked into a 13-14 defeat by Gala in their opening League game and that on their

Dave McIvor is halted by Steve Brotherstone as Edinburgh Academicals just fail to upset Melrose.

own patch. Gala then proceeded to play some of the most attractive rugby in the division under the coaching guidance of the former Grand Slam full-back Peter Dods to finish runner-up to the champions. Melrose simply bounced back to win their second game with ten tries and a 65-23 margin over Watsonians; then, with disaster facing them at 3-16 down to the powerful Edinburgh Academicals, they rallied for victory by 17-16, all their points being scored by the bubbling Gary Parker, from a try and four penalty goals. Parker thereafter dominated the points-scoring in the top two divisions with a massive haul of 190 points, including 11 tries from 13 games.

Although Melrose faced subsequent challenges from Stirling County, Gala, Heriot's FP and Edinburgh Academicals, the Greenyards side reeled off 12 wins on the trot and sealed the issue with a devastating display of the total game by running in 12 tries in their 74-10 margin over Edinburgh club Currie.

It was a mark of the type of game Melrose played that they scored 54 tries, 20 by their forwards, in their 13 games, 20 more than the runners-up, Gala. Only against Hawick did they fail to score a try, gaining their 12-10 win with four penalty goals by Parker to Hawick's two tries. The Melrose scrummage stood the strain and their 20-year-old prop, Millan Browne, gained selection for the South of Scotland and their 22-year-old hooker, Steven Brotherstone, was included in Scotland's tour to Argentina in May

and June. So, too, were Graham Shiel (seven caps), Carl Hogg (three caps) and scrum-half Bryan Redpath (three caps), as well as the 19-year-old wing Craig Joiner, who was in Scotland's squad at the Hong Kong Sevens. Doddie Weir was unavailable to tour and Craig Chalmers, who is likely now to stay with Melrose for next season, withdrew with knee ligament damage, otherwise Melrose would have had seven in the tour party.

Melrose were also ideally equipped for the increase in line-out play with four renowned ball-winners – Weir, Hogg, Ewan Simpson and Robbie Brown; and in the farmer Andrew Kerr, they had an open-side flanker of the old school, not of contemporary physical dimension but a dynamic type whose battery never seemed to run down. With three international players as their hinge – Bryan Redpath, Chalmers and Shiel – Melrose seldom lacked direction, and there was an ideal blend elsewhere with the robust, powerful running of centre Ross Brown (at 6 foot 3 almost as tall as his father, Peter, the former Scottish captain), the lightning acceleration of Joiner, the timely intrusion play of the rugged full-back, Craig Redpath, and the cheeky chappie craft of Parker.

Doddie Weir, more than head and shoulders above the rest.

It was a concern that their challengers failed to maintain the same consistent high quality of team play as Melrose, an aspect that has worried the Scottish Rugby Union, who thus introduced a series of matches between the Scottish districts and Irish provinces with a view to giving Scotland's cap aspirants a higher grade of challenge. And with the aim of heightening the intensity of club competition, the league system is likely to be restructured to incorporate three top divisions of eight clubs each, playing home and away, with thereafter seven divisions of ten clubs, a knock-out premiership and eventually a Scottish Cup.

Some former heavyweights found it hard to survive. Boroughmuir, champions in 1991, lost their first three games, and in mid-February were third from the bottom. Early in January Hawick were fourth from the foot but scored a notable away win over Stirling County by 12-8 in a run of four consecutive wins, including an astonishing 49-3 margin over Heriot's FP at Goldenacre.

Kelso and Selkirk were relegated, Selkirk, without a win, though they were one of the most exciting sides in the tables. They are succeeded by Glasgow High/Kelvinside, who won all 13 games as Division 2 champions, and Dundee High School FP, who were captained by Scotland's scrum-half, Andrew Nicol.

One intriguing factor about the 1994-95 campaign is how Melrose will fare in the absence of their coaching supremo, Jim Telfer, now the SRU's director of coaching. Telfer's drive and dedication, apart altogether from his planning and motivational gifts, will be sorely missed but he has imbued his younger disciples with the same qualities and principles, among them his likely successor, Rob Moffat, a schoolmaster who toured with Scotland as a wing in the Far East in 1977, and the inimitable Keith Robertson, whose own on-field daring used to give the watching Telfer some anxious moments!

Derrick Patterson moves the ball quickly for Edinburgh Academicals as Gary Hogg of Melrose closes in.

A LONG HARD SEASON
by David Stewart

The 1993-94 season was a long, hard one for the top club players in Wales, especially those who had international commitments. Frankly, it showed in the SWALEC Cup final in May. It would be quite wrong to deny Cardiff the merit of their 18-8 victory but there can be little doubt that there were a lot of tired players wearing the scarlet of Llanelli at the National Stadium that day. An incredible 14 members of their squad had represented Wales at full international level in the preceding year: Ieuan Evans had been with the Lions in New Zealand, large numbers of his team-mates went to Zimbabwe and Namibia with the international side; after an intense Heineken League programme and a full Cup schedule, many of them jetted off to Canada and the South Seas for the successful Welsh close-season tour. Their plight neatly focuses the biggest issue facing the game in Wales: that of professionalism in all its senses, not least the demands being made on leading players. As WRU chairman Vernon Pugh recently observed, the rules and administration of the sport must urgently make a differential allowance for two types of player: the few at the top end for whom rugby has become close to a full-time occupation, and the many at the lower end who play for fun.

It was a mixed, not to say confused season for Llanelli. In 12 months they went from doing the double to nothing. Surely international calls were not irrelevant in their finishing 13 points adrift of an outstanding Swansea squad in Heineken League Division 1? Stradey folk are proud of their contribution to the renewed Welsh success at international level, even if it meant the loss of their popular coach, Gareth Jenkins, who devoted his full attention to assisting Alan Davies with the national XV. Ieuan Evans captained Wales to the Championship; Scott Quinnell made a resounding impact in his first season, and Phil Davies, Ricky Evans, Mark Perego and Nigel Davies all made notable contributions. This year Llanelli provided the backbone of the national side. In the near future it may be Swansea or Neath or another leading club. How is the dilemma to be resolved? Already the major clubs carry squads of such a size that not all players can be given regular rugby.

The season ended on a couple of sour notes for Llanelli. Emyr Lewis went public on Welsh language TV about payments to players, and then refused to commit himself to the club for the following season. The new committee's decisive response was to drop him from the squad, apparently leaving Cardiff to pick up yet another back-row forward. The old committee was turfed out at a club general meeting, the main issue being the proposed sale of the club's famous car park (the destination of whose proceeds has been a matter of much speculation over the years, and is now the subject of Inland Revenue interest) due to financial problems. They are unlikely to struggle for long. The traditions of the club, and the special identity its players and supporters have with it, should see it through a turbulent period. An acid test was Ieuan Evans' decision to stay with them despite approaches from Harlequins and Cardiff.

Mike Budd of Cardiff moves in on Llanelli's Emyr Lewis in the Heineken League match which Llanelli won 15-9.

Whilst the problems of Llanelli are a microcosm of the challenges facing all leading Welsh clubs, to concentrate on them is unfair to Swansea. Few would deny that they were the best all-round team. The influence of Mike Ruddock, now a full-time director of coaching, continues to be immense. They won the Heineken League by four points from Neath having been without their skipper Stuart Davies for long periods and former star centre Scott Gibbs (due to an injury sustained in the Barbarians game initially; Rugby League thereafter). Their senior players served them well: Robert Jones (who spent the summer playing and coaching in Cape Town), vice-captain Tony Clement, and the old war-horse Richard Moriarty, whose spirit and love of the game see him go on and on. A new star was wing forward Rob Appleyard who, sadly, had to drop out of the South Seas tour as he had just been recruited into the police force.

Cardiff probably had to win something for their collective peace of mind. They have invested heavily in Alec Evans as coaching organiser, and more recently former outside-half Gareth Davies strolled down Cathedral Road from BBC Wales to take up his new position as chief executive at the club. A trio of Mikes were amongst their leading contributors: club captain Hall, playing the best rugby of his career; Rayer who regained his Welsh spot and whose club form showed a high level of consistency; Budd, one of many recruits from Bridgend over the years, whose big day at the Cup final was marred by an exceedingly nasty head wound (yes, sustained from a boot when he was on the ground – we would all prefer to see less of that).

Neath continued to occupy a unique slot on the scene. They also inspired great loyalty from their players. Skipper Gareth Llewellyn and farming prop John Davies never let the club down despite the demands of international rugby. Much praise is due to the young coaching team, including David Pickering, Kevin Phillips and Paul Thorburn (still doing his stuff from full-back), who have added a veneer of sophistication to the traditional rumbustious all-action style. Unfortunately, one of their unsung heroes, vertically challenged wing forward Adrian Varney, has elected to step down from First Division rugby because of working and family commitments.

Delight for Cardiff: captain Mike Hall raises the SWALEC Cup after their 15-8 win over Llanelli at the National Stadium.

The Neath style was emulated to a large degree by Pontypridd. In many ways their performance was the real success story of the season. Again, the ingredients appear to be a wise coach in Dennis John, an outstanding team spirit, and that little extra provided by star player Neil Jenkins, whose goal-kicking and general play was of a very high quality throughout. The club are delighted that eventually others such as Paul John, David Manley and Richie Collins have followed him into the national squad. Third place in the Heineken League, one point behind Neath, and a narrow semi-final defeat to Cardiff in the SWALEC Cup were fine achievements, and there will be little doubting their determination to secure some silverware next time. It is noticeable that their squad seems not to suffer from the summer 'musical chairs' in the way others do.

That is a problem which has afflicted Bridgend for more years now than they would care to recall. The heady days of the late 70s early 80s, when they were the strongest side in Wales, are now but a memory. In an attempt

Dunvant celebrate their arrival in Division 1 of the Heineken Leagues with a win over Newport.

to recapture the magic, former captain Steve Fenwick has been employed as the club's general manager. Primarily responsible for off-the-field activities, it is clear he will have a positive input on the playing side. His arrival has seen the departure of former director of coaching Clive Norling. The club were rightly annoyed at the suggestion (allegedly from a national selector) to Welsh squad wing Gwilym Wilkins that he should move to another club 'where he would get more ball' to improve his international prospects. Is it really good for the game in Wales if the international squad is drawn from essentially four or five clubs?

Like Bridgend, Newport predictably finished mid-table. They too have caught the bug for full-timers, in their case a chief executive. More troublingly, they haemorrhaged players from their squad during the close season, including promising lock Chris Wyatt.

Pontypool were at the 'Alamo' on successive Saturdays at the end of the season. They had to win twice to stay up, and they managed it by the skin of Bobby Windsor's teeth. His sacrifice in being present at their final League game spoke volumes for his loyalty to the club which put him at the top of the game. He was the only British Lion not to attend the reunion of the 1974 Lions in Northern Ireland because the dates clashed.

Mark Ring won admirers as outside-half/captain/backs coach. On the gammiest knee in Welsh rugby, he kept going when the going got tough and in doing so confounded a few cynics. Dunvant also survived, much to the joy of their ubiquitous chairman and local raconteur, Mr Dai Vaughan. It was only scoring difference which kept them up whilst Aberavon, the famous old Port Talbot club, suffered the ignominy of the drop, along with Cross Keys.

Their replacements in the First Division are Abertillery and Second Division champions Treorchy, whose storming season saw them win 20 games, draw one and lose only one.

Mountain Ash, coached by former British Lion Ian Stephens, went down along with Glamorgan Wanderers, recently of Division 1. Salt in the wound for Mountain Ash was provided by their near neighbours Abercynon replacing them along with West Glamorgan's Bonymaen. The changing of the guard further down saw St Peter's (giant-killers of Cardiff in the Cup 12 months earlier) and Dyfed club Tumble tumble down to the Fourth with Jeremy Pugh-inspired Builth Wells earning deserved promotion as the first genuine mid-Wales club in the Third Division alongside Caerphilly.

Treorchy provided one of the biggest talking-points of last season and, in their own way, are as much illustrative of what is happening in club rugby as are Llanelli. Readers of the local press have become used to stories reporting that this or that player has 'signed' for another club. The analogy with soccer is unmistakable. Officially it involved transfer forms; unofficially chequebooks. Treorchy, inspired by their energetic coach Clive Jones (ex-Loughborough University), have made their way thus far by harnessing the best local talent and promoting a strong identity with the famous Rhondda Valley which is their home. The suspicion is that they have now joined the 'rent-a-star' approach. For example, to achieve their lofty ambition of a top six place in their first Division 1 season they have recruited much-admired open-side flanker Lyn Jones (no known connection north of Porth).

Truly the game is becoming more 'professional' at club level with paid coaches and club managers, sport psychologists, intensive fitness training and dietary programmes, sponsored kit and players' cars, transfer forms, and the Inland Revenue offering immunity to Rugby League players to 'shop shamateurism' amongst their former colleagues of the Union game. There is much cleaning up to be done. The most amusing rumour following the season's end was that of the Gwent-based prop who, after signing transfer forms, discovered his cheque had bounced!

THE END OF AN ERA
by Chris Thau

By and large statistics are pretty unreliable. Besides, they tend to obscure the real facts rather than emphasise them: as they used to say, there are lies, damned lies and statistics. However, the fact that Toulouse have won the French Championship for the 11th time in their history to equal the record held by Béziers is quite significant, if not symbolic.

Toulouse, arguably the French club of the decade, have overcome their internal problems, triggered off by a conflict between the old management and the players, and have re-established themselves as the undisputed leader of the French domestic hierarchy. Conversely, Béziers, the darlings of the 1970s and the role-model for English clubs craving success 20 years ago, have been relegated to Group B, the French second division in every sense.

This is the end of an era in France. Béziers' demise has sent a shock wave into the heartland of French club rugby. If Béziers could go under, anybody could follow suit. And with the majority of the French clubs unable to balance their books, the example of the once-glorious Béziers – rapidly abandoned by its players – sends a shiver down the spine of most club presidents. Béziers have been followed into the B group by three other famous names: Mont-de-Marsan, Lourdes and Lyons student club (LOU).

Emile N'tamack on the break for Toulouse in their championship final against Montferrand.

Of the newly promoted, only Tyrosse have tasted the action in the first division before. The other three, Châteaurenard, Mandlieu and Saint Paul les Dax, have never been in the élite group before. They are all trying to strengthen their squads to cope with the tough life in the first division. New clubs, new money, new faces. The transfer market is booming. Everybody is looking for a new deal. The big names are in demand. Olivier Merle, the gigantic Grenoble lock, was offered a package he could not refuse by Montferrand. Romanian lock Cojocariu signed for SBUC only to return to Bayonne after much argument and of course 'incentive'. Merignac lost its entire front row, Laurent Seigne leaving for Brive, Serge Simon returning to Bordeaux, but SBUC rather than Bégles, and so on.

The tears in the eyes of the Montferrand captain, Philippe Saint-André, at the end of the French Championship final said it all – so near, yet so far. Toulouse at their best, orchestrated by the genius of Christophe Deylaud, proved too big a nut to crack for the warriors from Clermont-Ferrand. The dream finale of Toulon versus Toulouse failed to materialise when Montferrand delivered the killer blow (15-8) to Toulon in the quarter-finals. On their way to the final, Montferrand dispatched the second favourite – last year's finalists – Fouroux's gigantic Grenoble, but found out to their own chagrin that Toulouse have recaptured the magic, the power and the fluidity that makes them a unique club in France and one of the centres of rugby learning in the world.

Toulouse pose with their trophy after winning the French Championship.

A Summary of the Season
compiled by BILL MITCHELL

INTERNATIONAL RUGBY

Japan in Wales
September – October 1993

Opponents	Results	
Wales A	L	5 – 61
Dunvant	W	24 – 23
East Wales	L	12 – 38
West Wales	W	26 – 10
Heineken Select XV	W	39 – 10
WALES	L	5 – 55

Played 6 Won 3 Lost 3

Australia
in North America & France
October – November 1993

Opponents	Results	
USA Eagles	W	26 – 22
Canada B	W	40 – 3
CANADA	W	43 – 16
Aquitaine XV	W	30 – 15
South-West Selection	W	20 – 19
Languedoc-Roussillon	W	35 – 18
South-East France	W	24 – 23
FRANCE	L	13 – 16
Provence-Littoral XV	L	15 – 21
FRANCE	W	24 – 3
French Barbarians	W	43 – 26

Played 11 Won 9 Lost 2

South African Development in South America
October – November 1993

Opponents	Results	
Mar del Plata Selección	W	32 – 29
Chile	W	26 – 10
San Juan Selección	W	18 – 11
Argentina B	L	10 – 42
Santa Fe Selección	L	19 – 21
Uruguay	L	22 – 31

Played 6 Won 3 Lost 3

South Africa in Argentina
October – November 1993

Opponents	Results	
Provincial XV	W	55 – 37
Buenos Aires XV	L	27 – 28
Tucumán	W	40 – 12
ARGENTINA	W	29 – 26
Provincial XV	W	40 – 26
ARGENTINA	W	52 – 23

Played 6 Won 5 Lost 1

NEW ZEALAND IN ENGLAND, SCOTLAND & WALES

OCTOBER – DECEMBER 1993

Opponents	Results	
London Division	W	39 – 12
Midland Division	W	12 – 6
South-West Division	W	19 – 15
North Division	W	27 – 21
England A	W	26 – 12
South of Scotland	W	84 – 5
Scotland A	W	20 – 9
Scotland Dev'ment XV	W	31 – 12
SCOTLAND	W	51 – 15
England Emerging Players	W	30 – 19
England	L	9 – 15
Combined Services	W	13 – 3
Barbarians	W	25 – 10

Played 13 Won 12 Lost 1

AUCKLAND IN ENGLAND & SCOTLAND

NOVEMBER 1993

Opponents	Results	
Scottish Exiles	W	33 – 12
Edinburgh	W	27 – 21
Scottish Districts	L	19 – 24
Bedford	W	51 – 3
Bristol	W	44 – 7
West Hartlepool	W	34 – 8
Wasps	W	28 – 25

Played 7 Won 6 Lost 1

CANADA A IN ENGLAND & WALES

MARCH 1994

Opponents	Results	
North Division	L	8 – 18
Newbridge	W	9 – 8
Wales A	L	11 – 42
London Division	L	9 – 25
England Emerging Players	L	9 – 23

Played 5 Won 1 Lost 4

ENGLAND IN SOUTH AFRICA

MAY – JUNE 1994

Opponents	Results	
Orange Free State	L	11 – 22
Natal	L	6 – 21
Western Transvaal	W	26 – 24
Transvaal	L	21 – 24
South Africa A	L	16 – 19
SOUTH AFRICA	W	32 – 15
Eastern Province	W	31 – 13
SOUTH AFRICA	L	9 – 27

Played 8 Won 3 Lost 5

Ireland
in Australia
May – June 1994

Opponents	Results
Western Australia	W 64 – 8
New South Wales	L 18 – 55
ACT	L 9 – 22
Queensland	L 26 – 29
Australian XV	L 9 – 57
AUSTRALIA	L 13 – 33
NSW Country	W 20 – 18
AUSTRALIA	L 18 – 32

Played 8 Won 2 Lost 6

Wales World Cup Matches & Summer Tour
May – June 1994

Opponents	Results
PORTUGAL (RWC)	W 102 – 11
SPAIN (RWC)	W 54 – 0
Canadian Select XV	W 28 – 19
CANADA	W 33 – 15
FIJI	W 23 – 8
TONGA	W 18 – 9
WESTERN SAMOA	L 9 – 34

Played 7 Won 6 Lost 1

Scotland
in Argentina
May – June 1994

Opponents	Results
Buenos Aires Seleccion	D 24 – 24
Cuyo	L 11 – 25
Cordoba	W 40 – 14
ARGENTINA	L 15 – 16
Rosario	L 16 – 27
ARGENTINA	L 17 – 19

Played 6 Won 1 Drawn 1 Lost 4

Barbarians
in Zimbabwe
May – June 1994

Opponents	Results
Goshawks	W 53 – 9
Matabeleland	W 35 – 23
Zimbabwe	L 21 – 23

Played 3 Won 2 Lost 1

ITALY
IN AUSTRALIA
JUNE 1994

Opponents	Results	
South Australia	W	60 – 12
Sydney XV	W	36 – 26
Queensland XV	W	21 – 19
Queensland Country	W	57 – 13
AUSTRALIA	L	20 – 23
New South Wales	W	30 – 20
AUSTRALIA	L	7 – 20

Played 7 Won 5 Lost 2

FRANCE
IN CANADA & NEW ZEALAND
JUNE – JULY 1994

Opponents	Results	
Canada A	W	34 – 31
CANADA	L	16 – 18
North Auckland	W	28 – 23
North Harbour	L	23 – 27
Wairarapa-Bush	W	53 – 9
New Zealand A	W	33 – 25
Nelson Bays	W	46 – 18
NEW ZEALAND	W	20 – 8
Hawke's Bay	L	25 – 30
NEW ZEALAND	W	23 – 20

Played 10 Won 7 Lost 3

SOUTH AFRICA
IN NEW ZEALAND
JUNE – AUGUST 1994

Opponents	Results	
King Country	W	46 – 10
Counties	W	37 – 26
Wellington	W	36 – 26
Southland	W	51 – 15
Hanan Shield XV	W	67 – 19
NEW ZEALAND	L	14 – 22
Taranaki	W	16 – 12
Waikato	W	38 – 17
Manawatu	W	47 – 21
NEW ZEALAND	L	9 – 13
Otago	L	12 – 19
Canterbury	W	21 – 11
Bay of Plenty	W	33 – 12
NEW ZEALAND	D	18 – 18

Played 14 Won 10 Drawn 1 Lost 3

WESTERN SAMOA
IN AUSTRALIA
JULY – AUGUST 1994

Opponents	Results	
Victoria	W	60 – 26
ACT	W	39 – 13
Queensland	W	24 – 22
New South Wales XV	W	21 – 18
AUSTRALIA	L	3 – 73

Played 5 Won 4 Lost1

SUPER-10 TOURNAMENT
IN SOUTH AFRICA
MAY 1993

POOL A

	P	W	L	F	A	Pts
Queensland	4	3	1	116	63	6
N Harbour	4	3	1	83	59	6
Otago	4	2	2	119	109	4
Transvaal	4	2	2	104	97	4
E Province	4	0	4	70	164	0

POOL B

	P	W	L	F	A	Pts
Natal	4	4	0	92	62	8
NSW	4	3	1	90	58	6
W Samoa	4	2	2	96	104	4
Auckland	4	1	3	71	61	2
Waikato	4	0	4	68	132	0

Final
Natal 10 Queensland 21

BLEDISLOE CUP 1994

Australia 20 New Zealand 16

THE FIVE NATIONS
CHAMPIONSHIP
1994

Results

France	35	Ireland	15
Wales	29	Scotland	6
Ireland	15	Wales	17
Scotland	14	England	15
England	12	Ireland	13
Wales	24	France	15
France	14	England	18
Ireland	6	Scotland	6
England	15	Wales	8
Scotland	12	France	20

	P	W	D	L	F	A	Pts
Wales	4	3	0	1	78	51	6
England	4	3	0	1	60	49	6
France	4	2	0	2	84	69	4
Ireland	4	1	1	2	49	70	3
Scotland	4	0	1	3	38	70	1

CATHAY PACIFIC-HONGKONG
BANK SEVENS
1994

Cup Final
New Zealand 32 Australia 20
Plate Final
US Eagles 21 South Korea 26
Bowl Final
Hong Kong 24 Portugal 12

OTHER INTERNATIONAL MATCHES
1993-94

Results

England U21	37	Italy U21	12
New Zealand	35	Western Samoa	15
France	51	Romania	0
England U21	22	Ireland U21	15
Wales	24	Canada	26
Ireland	25	Romania	3
Italy	18	Scotland A	15
Scotland A	24	Ireland A	9
Wales U21	36	Scotland U21	0
Ireland A	10	Wales A	20
Italy A	9	England A	15
Spain	17	England Emerging Players	86
England A	29	Ireland A	14
France A	9	Scotland A	12
France A	20	England A	8
Wales A	21	France A	8
Holland	14	England A	56
France U21	13	England U21	9
Romania U21	8	Wales U21	12
United States	10	Canada	15

BARBARIAN FC
1993-94

Opponents	Results	
Exeter	W	59 – 14
Newport	L	19 – 35
New Zealand	L	12 – 25
Leicester	L	14 – 51
East Midlands	W	55 – 25
Cardiff	W	53 – 27
Swansea	L	31 – 51
Goshawks	W	53 – 9
Matabeleland	W	35 – 23
Zimbabwe	L	21 – 23

Played 10 won 5 lost 5

CLUB, COUNTY AND DIVISIONAL RUGBY

ENGLAND

Pilkington Cup
Quarter-finals

Gloucester	3	Orrell	10
Harlequins	26	Sale	13
Leicester	12	Moseley	6
Saracens	6	Bath	23

Semi-finals

Harlequins	25	Bath	26
Orrell	18	Leicester	31

Final

Bath	21	Leicester	9

Pilkington Shield Final

Malvern	8	O Hamptonians	6

Courage Leagues
Division 1

	P	W	D	L	F	A	Pts
Bath	18	17	0	1	431	181	34
Leicester	18	14	0	4	425	210	28
Wasps	18	10	1	7	362	340	21
Bristol	18	10	0	8	331	276	20
Northampton	18	9	0	9	305	342	18
Harlequins	18	8	0	10	333	287	16
Orrell	18	8	0	10	327	302	16
Gloucester	18	6	2	10	247	356	14
London Irish	18	4	0	14	217	391	8
N'castle Gos	18	2	1	15	190	483	5

Division 2

	P	W	D	L	F	A	Pts
Sale	18	13	2	3	438	160	28
W Hartlepool	18	13	2	3	389	271	28
Saracens	18	11	1	6	299	238	23
Wakefield	18	8	3	7	347	240	19
Moseley	18	9	1	8	266	220	19
Nottingham	18	8	1	9	254	326	17
Waterloo	18	6	2	10	231	346	14
Ldn Scottish	18	6	0	12	232	325	12
Rugby	18	5	1	12	186	302	11
Otley	18	4	1	13	235	449	9

Division 3 champions: Coventry
Runners-up: Fylde
Division 4: Clifton

Division 5 North: Rotherham
Division 5 South: Reading

CIS County Championship
Semi-finals

Cornwall	9	Durham	14
Yorkshire	13	Gloucestershire	12

Final

Durham	3	Yorkshire	26

CIS Divisional Championship

	P	W	D	L	F	A	Pts
South & S-W	3	3	0	0	85	36	6
London	3	2	0	1	62	60	4
North	3	1	0	2	68	60	2
Midlands	3	0	0	3	26	85	0

University Match

Oxford Univ	20	Cambridge Univ	8

University Second Teams Match

Oxford Univ	20	Cambridge Univ	23

University Under-21 Match

Oxford Univ	10	Cambridge Univ	12

UAU Cup Final

Northumbria	13	West London	9

Hospitals Cup

Charing X/Westm'ster	18	St Mary's	19

Inter-Services Champions: Royal Air Force
Securicor Trophy: British Police
Middlesex Sevens Champions: Bath
National Tens Champions: Bristol

WALES

SWALEC Welsh Challenge Cup
Quarter-finals
Cardiff	20	SW Police	13
Maesteg	35	Tenby United	7
Neath	3	Llanelli	7
Pontypridd	32	Newbridge	10

Semi-finals
Cardiff	8	Pontypridd	6
Llanelli	23	Maesteg	7

Final
Cardiff	15	Llanelli	8

Heineken Leagues
Division 1
	P	W	D	L	F	A	Pts
Swansea	22	20	0	2	549	264	40
Neath	22	17	2	3	581	286	36
Pontypridd	22	17	1	4	571	299	35
Cardiff	22	15	2	5	668	240	32
Llanelli	22	13	1	8	461	366	27
Bridgend	22	10	1	11	466	434	21
Newport	22	8	2	12	362	472	18
Newbridge	22	7	1	14	367	440	15
Pontypool	22	7	0	15	312	626	14
Dunvant	22	6	1	15	288	464	13
Aberavon	22	6	1	15	242	464	13
Cross Keys	22	0	0	22	239	751	0

Division 2
	P	W	D	L	F	A	Pts
Treorchy	22	20	1	1	425	200	41
Abertillery	22	15	1	6	473	242	31
Maesteg	22	13	1	8	376	259	27
S Wales Pol	22	12	0	10	367	333	24
Tenby Utd	22	10	0	12	308	366	20
Llanharan	22	9	2	11	259	349	20
Narberth	22	10	0	12	273	294	20
Penarth	22	9	0	13	291	372	18
Ebbw Vale	22	8	2	12	279	321	18
Llandovery	22	8	1	13	269	370	17
Mountain A	22	8	0	14	275	333	16
Glam Wdrs	22	6	0	16	262	418	12

Division 3 champions: Abercynon
Runners-up: Bonymaen
Division 4 champions: Builth Wells
Runners-up: Caerphilly

SCOTLAND

McEwan's Inter-District Championship
Semi-finals
Glasgow	21	Edinburgh	6
South	37	North & Midlands	13

Third Place
Edinburgh	28	North & Midlands	25

Final
South	28	Glasgow	14

Alloa Brewery Cup Final
Boroughmuir	42	Dundee HSFP	18

Castlemaine XXXX Trophy Final
Forester FP	22	Garnock	6

McEwan's National Leagues
Division 1
	P	W	D	L	F	A	Pts
Melrose	13	12	0	1	410	192	24
Gala	12	9	0	3	274	214	18
Edinb'gh Ac	13	8	1	4	265	183	17
Heriot's FP	12	7	0	5	230	224	14
Watsonians	13	7	0	6	276	337	14
Stirling Co	12	6	1	5	227	163	13
Hawick	12	6	1	5	218	178	13
Jed-Forest	13	6	0	7	231	199	12
Currie	12	6	0	6	230	285	12
Stewart's/M	13	5	1	7	157	190	11
Boroughmuir	12	5	0	7	214	228	10
W of Scotland	13	4	1	8	235	279	9
Kelso	13	4	0	9	175	296	8
Selkirk	13	0	1	12	138	312	1

Division 2
	P	W	D	L	F	A	Pts
G'gow H/K	13	13	0	0	440	115	26
Dundee HSFP	12	11	0	1	395	80	22
Kirkcaldy	13	10	0	3	277	150	20
Edinburgh W	13	8	0	5	214	251	16
Musselburgh	13	7	0	6	204	185	14
Peebles	13	6	0	7	206	219	12
Glasgow Ac	13	5	1	7	237	276	11
Wigtownshire	13	5	0	8	172	241	10
Haddington	12	5	0	7	146	220	10
Grangemouth	13	4	1	8	201	293	9
Biggar	13	3	2	8	203	240	8
Preston L FP	13	4	0	9	158	291	8
Clarkston	13	4	0	9	158	357	8
Ayr	13	3	0	10	168	261	6

Division 3 champions: Gordonians
Runners-up: Corstorphine
Division 4 champions: Trinity Academicals
Runners-up: Edinburgh University

IRELAND

Insurance Corporation All-Ireland Leagues
Division 1

	P	W	D	L	F	A	Pts
Garryowen	10	8	0	2	172	108	16
Cork Const	10	7	0	3	201	123	14
Blackrock	10	7	0	3	137	99	14
Dungannon	10	5	0	5	181	130	10
Lansdowne	10	5	0	5	162	167	10
St Mary's	10	5	0	5	157	163	10
Y Munster	10	5	0	5	102	149	10
Shannon	10	4	0	6	107	104	8
Old Wesley	10	4	0	6	114	138	8
Greystones	10	4	0	6	97	156	8
Wanderers	10	1	0	9	141	234	2

Division 2

	P	W	D	L	F	A	Pts
Instonians	10	8	0	2	205	100	20
Sun's Well	10	8	0	2	184	118	16
Ballymena	10	7	0	3	214	125	14
Old B'vedere	10	7	0	3	141	125	14
Bangor	10	5	0	5	122	189	10
Terenure	10	4	1	5	149	112	9
Malone	10	4	1	5	125	141	9
Old Crescent	10	4	0	6	173	150	8
Dolphin	10	4	0	6	139	144	8
Galwegians	10	3	0	7	113	124	6
Ballina	10	0	0	10	72	309	0

Inter-Provincial Championship

	P	W	D	L	F	A	Pts
Leinster	4	3	0	1	72	40	6
Ulster	4	3	0	1	84	59	6
Munster	4	3	0	1	91	71	6
Exiles	4	1	0	3	72	80	2
Connacht	4	0	0	4	42	111	0

Senior Provincial Cup Finals
Leinster:
Terenure College 12 Greystones 8
Munster:
Sunday's Well 20 Young Munster 9
Ulster:
Dungannon 14 Instonians 10
Connacht:
Corinthians 14 Connemara 10

FRANCE

French Club Championship
Semi-finals
Toulouse 30 Dax 25
Montferrand 22 Grenoble 15
Final
Toulouse 22 Montferrand 16

The Whitbread
Rugby World
Annual Awards

Player of the Year	Ben Clarke (Bath)
International Player of the Year	Tim Horan (Queensland)
Senior Team of the Year	Bath RFC
Most Promising Player	Scott Quinnell (Llanelli)
Junior Club of the Year	Esher RFC
The Photograph of the Year	David Gibson
For Services to Journalism	Clem Thomas
Coach of the Year	Alan Davies
Referee of the Year	Derek Bevan
Youth Team of the Year	Pontypridd Youth
School of the Year	Millfield School

1

2

3

4

Whitbread *Rugby World* Monthly Awards

November 1993
Player of the Month	Jonathan Callard (Bath)
Senior Club	Gala
Junior Club	Nottingham Casuals

December 1993
Player of the Month	Victor Ubogu (Bath)
Senior Club	West Hartlepool
Junior Club	Kettering

January 1994
Player of the Month	Nigel Redman (Bath)
Senior Club	Treorchy (Rhondda)
Junior Club	Ealing

February 1994
Player of the Month	Rob Andrew (Wasps)
Senior Club	Sale
Junior Club	Sandal

March 1994
Player of the Month	Neil Jenkins (Pontypridd)
Senior Club	Ystradgynlais
Junior Club	Taunton

April 1994
Player of the Month	Scott Quinnell (Llanelli)
Senior Club	Melrose
Junior Club	Hucclecote Old Boys

May 1994
Player of the Month	Dean Richards (Leicester)
Senior Club	Clifton
Junior Club	Esher

1. Ben Clarke
2. Scott Quinnell
3. Tim Horan
4. Bath RFC
5. Derek Bevan
6. Andy Cooke – Esher RFC
7. Alan Davies
8. David Gibson
9. Clem Thomas

5

6

7

8

9

FIXTURES
1994-95

AUGUST 1994

Sat 27th   Heineken Leagues (1) Divs 1 & 2
           Selkirk Sevens

SEPTEMBER 1994

Sat 3rd   Bath v Barbarians (Centenary Match)
           Heineken Leagues (2) Divs 1 & 2
           Heineken Leagues (1) Divs 3 to 5
Sun 4th   Kelso Sevens
Tue 6th   French Barbarians v Barbarians
Wed 7th   Heineken Leagues (3) Divs 1 & 2
Sat 10th   Courage Leagues (1) Divs 1 & 2
           Courage Leagues (1) Divs 3 & 4
           Pilkington Cup Round 1
           Pilkington Shield Round 1
           Heineken Leagues (2) Divs 3 to 5
           McEwan's Leagues (1)
Sat 17th   Romania v Wales (World Cup)
           Courage Leagues (2) Divs 1 & 2
           Courage Leagues (2) Divs 3 & 4
           Courage Leagues (1) All others
           SWALEC Cup Round 1
           Heineken Leagues (3) Divs 3 to 5
           McEwan's Leagues (2)
           Insurance Corporation Leagues (1) 1 to 4
Sat 24th   Courage Leagues (3) Divs 1 & 2
           Courage Leagues (3) Divs 3 & 4
           Courage Leagues (2) All others
           Heineken Leagues (4) Divs 1 to 4
           McEwan's Leagues (3)
           Insurance Corporation Leagues (2) 1 to 4
Sun 25th   Insurance Corporation Leagues Div 1:
           Garryowen v Shannon

OCTOBER 1994

Sat 1st   Italy v Romania (World Cup)
           Courage Leagues (4) Divs 1 & 2
           Courage Leagues (4) Divs 3 & 4
           Courage Leagues (3) All others
           Heineken Leagues (5) Divs 1 to 4
           Heineken Leagues (4) Div 5
           McEwan's Leagues (4)
           Insurance Corporation Leagues (3) 1 to 4
Tue 4th   Newport v Barbarians
Sat 8th   Courage Leagues (5) Divs 1 & 2
           Pilkington Cup Round 2
           Pilkington Shield Round 2
           Heineken Leagues (6) Divs 3 & 4
           Heineken Leagues (5) Div 5
           McEwan's Leagues (5)
           Insurance Corporation Leagues (4) 1 to 4
Sun 9th   Insurance Corporation Leagues Div 1:
           Young Munster v Garryown
Wed 12th   Wales v Italy (World Cup)
Sat 15th   Courage Leagues (6) Divs 1 & 2
           Courage Leagues (5) Divs 3 & 4
           Courage Leagues (4) All others
           Heineken Leagues (6) Divs 1 & 2
           Heineken Leagues (7) Divs 3 & 4
           Heineken Leagues (6) Div 5
           McEwan's Leagues (6)
           Insurance Corporation Leagues (5) 1 to 4
Sun 16th   Insurance Corporation Leagues Div 1:
           Sunday's Well v Shannon
Sat 22nd   Cardiff v South Africa
           Courage Leagues (7) Divs 1 & 2
           Courage Leagues (6) Divs 3 & 4
           Courage Leagues (5) All others
           SWALEC Cup Round 2
           Heineken Leagues (8) Divs 3 & 4
           Scotland & Ireland Dist & Prov
           matches:
           South of Scotland v Ulster
           Glasgow v Leinster
           Connacht v North & Midlands
           Munster v Edinburgh
Wed 26th   Wales A v South Africa
Sat 29th   Llanelli v South Africa
           Courage Leagues (8) Divs 1 & 2
           Courage Leagues (7) Divs 3 & 4

Courage Leagues (6) All others
Heineken Leagues (7) Divs 1 & 2
Heineken Leagues (9) Divs 3 & 4
Heineken Leagues (7) Div 5
Scotland & Ireland Dist & Prov
   matches:
   Leinster v South of Scotland
   Ulster v Glasgow
   North & Midlands v Munster
   Edinburgh v Connacht

NOVEMBER 1994

Tue 1st	Irish Development XV v Namibia
Wed 2nd	Neath v South Africa
Thu 4th	Bridgend v Canterbury
Sat 5th	Ireland v Namibia
	Swansea v South Africa
	Oxford University v Romania
	Courage Leagues (9) Divs 1 & 2
	Pilkington Cup Round 3
	Pilkington Shield Round 3
	Heineken Leagues (8) Divs 1 & 2
	Heineken Leagues (10) Divs 3 & 4
	Heineken Leagues (8) Div 5
	McEwan's Leagues (7)
Mon 7th	Leinster v Canterbury
Tue 8th	Cambridge University v Romania
Wed 9th	Scotland A v South Africa
	Irish Universities v Namibia
	Cornwall v Canterbury
Sat 12th	England v Romania
	Scottish Combined Districts v South Africa
	Leinster v Namibia
	Courage Leagues (8) Divs 3 & 4
	West Hartlepool v Canterbury
	Heineken Leagues (9) Divs 1 & 2
	Heineken Leagues (10) Divs 3 & 4
	Heineken Leagues (9) Div 5
	Irish Inter-provincial matches:
	Munster v Ulster
	Connacht v Exiles
Tue 15th	Scottish Selection v South Africa
	Moseley v Canterbury
Wed 16th	Oxford University v R. V. Stanley's XV
Thu 17th	Coventry v Canterbury
Sat 19th	Scotland v South Africa

Divisional Championship :
   South-West v London & SE
   North v Midlands
County Championship
   Gloucester v Canterbury
SWALEC Cup Round 3
Heineken Leagues (10) Divs 1 & 2
Irish Inter-provincial matches:
   Leinster v Exiles
   Ulster v Connacht

Tue 22nd	Pontypridd v South Africa
	Bristol v Canterbury
Wed 23rd	Cambridge University v Steele-Bodger's XV
Fri 25th	Ulster v Canterbury
Sat 26th	Wales v South Africa
	Divisional championship
	London & SE v North
	Midlands v South-West
	County Championship matches
	Pilkington Shield Round 4
	McEwan's Leagues (8)
	Irish Inter-provincial matches:
	Exiles v Munster
	Connacht v Leinster
Tue 29th	Combined Irish Provinces v South Africa

DECEMBER 1994

Sat 3rd	Barbarians v South Africa
	Divisional Championship:
	London & SE v Midlands
	North v South-West
	County Championship matches
	Heineken Leagues (11) Divs 1 & 2
	Heineken Leagues (12) Divs 3 & 4
	Heineken Leagues (10) Div 5
	Scottish Inter-district matches:
	South v Scottish Exiles
	Glasgow v North & Midlands
Tue 6th	Oxford v Cambridge
	Oxford v Cambridge Under-21s
	England Emerging Players v Canada
Sat 10th	England v Canada
	County Championship matches
	Heineken Leagues (12) Divs 1 & 2
	Heineken Leagues (13) Divs 3 & 4

Heineken Leagues (11) Div 5
Scottish Inter-district matches:
  North & Midlands v Edinburgh
  Scottish Exiles v Glasgow
Irish Inter-provincial matches
  Exiles v Ulster
  Leinster v Munster
Wed 14th   Scottish Inter-district match:
  South v Edinburgh
Sat 17th   Pilkington Cup Round 4
  Pilkington Shield Round 5
  SWALEC Cup Round 4
  Scottish Inter-district matches:
    Edinburgh v Glasgow
    North & Midlands v South
  Irish Inter-provincial matches:
    Ulster v Leinster
    Munster v Connacht
Wed 21st   Scottish Inter-district match:
  Scottish Exiles v North & Midlands
Sat 24th   Heineken Leagues (13) Divs 1 & 2
  Scottish Inter-district matches:
    Glasgow v South
    Edinburgh v Scottish Exiles
Tue 27th   Leicester v Barbarians
Sat 31st   Scotland International Trial
  Heineken Leagues (14) Divs 1 & 2

JANUARY 1995
Sat 7th   Scotland A v Italy
  Courage Leagues (10) Divs 1 & 2
  Courage Leagues (9) Divs 3 & 4
  Courage Leagues (7) All others
  Heineken Leagues (15) Divs 1 & 2
  Heineken Leagues (14) Divs 3 & 4
  Heineken Leagues (12) Div 5
  Insurance Corporation Leagues (6) 1 to 4
Sun 8th   Insurance Corporation Leagues Div 1:
  Garryowen v Sunday's Well
Sat 14th   Courage Leagues (11) Divs 1 & 2
  Courage Leagues (10) Divs 3 & 4
  Courage Leagues (8) All others
  Heineken Leagues (15) Divs 3 & 4
  Heineken Leagues (13) Div 5
  McEwan's Leagues (9)
  Insurance Corporation Leagues (7) 1 to 4
Fri 20th   Ireland A v England A
  Ireland Students v England Students

Sat 21st   Ireland v England
  France v Wales
  Scotland A v France A
Sat 28th   Pilkington Cup Round 5
  Pilkington Shield Round 6
  SWALEC Cup Round 5
  McEwan's Leagues (10)

FEBRUARY 1995
Fri 3rd   England A v France A
  Scotland A v Ireland A
  Scotland v Ireland (Under-21s)
  England Students v French Students
Sat 4th   England v France
  Scotland v Ireland
  Heineken Leagues (16) Divs 1 to 4
  Heineken Leagues (14) Div 5
Tue/Wed
7th/8th   Heineken Leagues (17) Divs 1 & 2
Sat 11th   Courage Leagues (12) Divs 1 & 2
  Courage Leagues (11) Divs 3 & 4
  Courage Leagues (9) All others
  Heineken Leagues (17) Divs 3 & 4
  Heineken Leagues (15) Divs 5 Wal)
  McEwan's Leagues (11)
  Insurance Corporation Leagues (8) 1 to 4
Sun 12th   Insurance Corporation Leagues Div 1:
  Cork Constitution v Shannon
Fri 17th   France A v Wales A
  France v Scotland (Under-21s)
  Wales Students v England Students
Sat 18th   Wales v England
  France v Scotland
  Insurance Corporation Leagues (9) 1 to 4
Sat 25th   Pilkington Cup Quarter-finals
  Pilkington Shield Quarter-finals
  Courage Leagues (12) Divs 3 & 4
  Courage Leagues (10) All others
  Heineken Leagues (18) Divs 1 to 4
  Heineken Leagues (16) Div 5
  McEwan's Leagues (12)
  Insurance Corporation Leagues
    Div 3:
    Highfield v University College Cork
    Div 4:
    Queen's University, Belfast v Sligo
    University College Galway v Dublin
    University

MARCH 1995

Fri 3rd	Scotland v Wales (Under-21s)
	Heineken Leagues (19) Div 3
Sat 4th	Scotland v Wales
	Ireland v France
	Courage Leagues (13) Divs 1 & 2
	Courage Leagues (13) Divs 3 & 4
	Courage Leagues (11) All others
Wed 8th	East Midlands v Barbarians
Sat 11th	County Championship Semi-finals
	Heineken Leagues (19) Divs 1,2 & 4
	Heineken Leagues (17) Div 5
	McEwan's Leagues (13)
	Insurance Corporation Leagues (10) 1 to 4
Sun 12th	Insurance Corporation Leagues Div 1:
	Sunday's Well v Cork Constitution
Fri 17th	Wales A v Ireland A
	Wales v Ireland (Under 21's)
	England Students v Italy Students
Sat 18th	England v Scotland
	Wales v Ireland
Sun 19th	England A v Italy A
Wed 22nd	British Universities Sports Association
	Final
Sat/Sun 25/26	Cathay Pacific/HongkongBank Sevens
Sat 25th	Courage Leagues (14) Divs 1 & 2
	Courage Leagues (14) Divs 3 & 4
	Courage Leagues (12) All others
	Daily Mail Schools Day
	SWALEC Cup Round 5
	Heineken Leagues (18) Div 5
	McEwan's Leagues stand-by day

APRIL 1995

Sat 1st	Pilkington Cup Semi-finals
	Pilkington Shield Semi-finals
	Courage Leagues (15) Divs 3 & 4
	Royal Navy v Army
	Heineken Leagues (20) Divs 1 to 4
	Heineken Leagues (19) Div 5
	Insurance Corporation Leagues (11) 1 to 4
	Gala Sevens
	Scotland v Italy (Under-21s)
	Spain v Scotland (Under-18s)
Sat 8th	Courage Leagues (15) Divs 1 & 2
	Courage Leagues (16) Divs 3 & 4

	Courage Leagues (13) All others
	SWALEC Cup Quarter-finals
	Heineken Leagues (20) Div 5
	Melrose Sevens
	Scotland v England (Under-19s)
	Scotland v Ireland (Under-18s)
Wed 12th	Army v Royal Air Force
Sat 15th	Courage Leagues (15) Divs 1 & 2
	Courage Leagues (16) Divs 3 & 4
	Cardiff v Barbarians 4
	Heineken Leagues (21) Divs 1 to 5
	Hawick Sevens
	Scotland v Wales (Under-19s)
Sun 16th	Earlston Sevens
Mon 17th	Swansea v Barbarians
Wed 19th	Royal Navy v Royal Air Force
Sat 22nd	County Championship Final
	County Championship Under-21s Final
	Courage Leagues (17) Divs 1 & 2
	SWALEC Cup Semi-finals
	Jed-Forest Sevens
Sat 29th	Courage Leagues (18) Divs 1 & 2
	Courage Leagues (18) Divs 3 & 4
	Heineken Leagues (22) Divs 1 to 5
	Langholm Sevens

MAY 1995

Sat 6th	Pilkington Cup Final
	Pilkington Shield Final
	SWALEC Cup Final
	France v Wales (Under-21s)
Sat 13th	Middlesex Sevens Finals

RUGBY WORLD CUP

MAY 1995

	POOL	
Thu 25th	A	Australia v South Africa (Cape Town)
Fri 26th	D	Scotland v Ivory Coast (Rustenburg)
	D	France v Tonga (Pretoria)
	A	Canada v Europe 3 (Port Elizabeth)
Sat 27th	B	Western Samoa v Europe 2 (East London)
	B	England v Argentina (Durban)
	C	Europe 1 v Asia (Bloemfontein)
	C	New Zealand v Ireland (Johannesburg)
Tue 30th	A	South Africa v Europe 3 (Cape Town)
	B	Western Samoa v Argentina (East London)
	D	France v Ivory Coast (Rustenburg)
	D	Scotland v Tonga (Pretoria)
Wed 31st	A	Australia v Canada (Port Elizabeth)
	B	England v Europe 2 (Durban)
	C	Ireland v Asia (Bloemfontein)
	C	New Zealand v Europe 1 (Johannesburg)

JUNE 1995

Sat 3rd	A	Australia v Europe 3 (Stellenbosch)
	A	Canada v South Africa (Port Elizabeth)
	D	Tonga v Ivory Coast (Rustenburg)
	D	Scotland v France (Pretoria)
Sun 4th	B	Argentina v Europe 2 (East London)
	B	England v Western Samoa (Durban)
	C	New Zealand v Asia (Bloemfontein)
	C	Ireland v Europe (Johannesburg)
Sat 10th	E	Winners D v Runners-up C (Durban)
	F	Winners A v Runners-up B (Johannesburg)
Sun 11th	H	Winners B v Runners-up A (Cape Town)
	G	Winners C v Runners-up D (Pretoria)
Sat 17th		Semi-final Winners E v Winners F (Durban)
Sun 18th		Semi-final Winners G v Winners H (Cape Town)
Thu 22nd		Third-place play-off (Pretoria)
Sat 24th		**FINAL** (Johannesburg)